Teaching clever children, 7–11

Teaching
clever children, 7–11

N. R. Tempest

Emeritus Professor of Education
University of Liverpool

Routledge & Kegan Paul

London and Boston

First published in 1974
by Routledge & Kegan Paul Ltd
Broadway House, 68–74 Carter Lane,
London EC4V 5EL and
9 Park Street,
Boston, Mass. 02108, U.S.A.
Printed in Great Britain by
Unwin Brothers Limited
The Gresham Press
Old Woking, Surrey
and set in Monotype Times
© N. R. Tempest, 1974

ISBN 0 7100 7805 6 (c)
ISBN 0 7100 7806 4 (p)

Library of Congress Catalog
Card No. 73-91039

Contents

Preface

The study described in this book was made possible by the generous financial support of the Leverhulme Trust Fund, to whose Director and Trustees the author and his colleagues offer their sincere gratitude. Grateful thanks are also due to the Southport Education Committee, the Chief Education Officer, Mr K. Robinson and the headmaster, Mr G. R. Gamble, and the staff of the school which received the children, for their whole-hearted co-operation. Grateful mention must also be made of the late Mr S. R. Hutton who was Southport's Chief Education Officer when the study began. Our thanks go to the parents who entrusted their children to us, for their forbearance and understanding over four years.

The original testing was undertaken by final honours students of the University of Liverpool Department of Psychology, through the kindness of Professor L. S. Hearnshaw, under the direction of two members of the staff of the School of Education, D. G. Pritchard, now Professor of Education, University College, Swansea, and D. J. Thomas, senior lecturer in special education.

In addition to the author, who was responsible for the project, the members of the team were: R. W. Callow, class teacher; R. R. Stewart, educational psychologist; R. Derricott, lecturer in education in the University of Liverpool who taught science; Miss P. M. Alston, music; Mrs E. M. J. Gray (first year) and Mrs L. Coates (second and third years), German. Chapters 3, 4, 5 and 6 are written from reports of their work by the teachers concerned, but the author is responsible for the other chapters and for the final text of the book and any errors or omissions are his.

Introduction

This book is addressed particularly to teachers and others who are concerned with the education of young children between the ages of seven and eleven. Among these children, the clever and the backward, at the two extremes of ability, are likely to present problems in a school class of thirty or more. The difficulties of the backward and the slow learners have been widely studied, but little attention has yet been paid in Great Britain to the clever children who make up 2 or 3 per cent of their age group. It is commonly believed that such children have no educational problems, that they do everything easily and well and share the satisfaction of teachers and parents in their performance. We believe that those who do well are not necessarily satisfied but are bored if their work is not sufficiently challenging, and that others do not do well, either because their abilities remain undiscovered, or because they are unsuited to the kind of education offered. There appeared to be two key questions: how are clever children to be recognized at the early age of seven? and how can their abilities be challenged in school? One way of finding answers was to bring together some clever seven-year-old children and observe and teach them for four years until they moved into secondary schools. This, in essence, was the project undertaken by the Liverpool University School of Education on which this book is based.

In the summer of 1967 about 1,000 children, aged seven, in their last term in the infant schools of a seaside town were given a group test of intelligence (Young, 1966) and their teachers were asked to name those they thought 'gifted' according to a few simple criteria. As a result of the test, about 100 children appeared with IQ 127 or above and these were individually tested by means of a shortened form of the Wechsler Intelligence Scale for Children, a Schonell Word Recognition Test and a series of items designed to measure fluency, flexibility and originality, the qualities of thought commonly termed 'divergent thinking' or 'creativity'. Following these tests, the consent of the parents of fifteen children with IQ 130 upwards and an average of 140 was obtained to their being formed into a small class in a centrally situated primary school. There they would stay for the next four years until they moved into secondary schools in the autumn of 1971. The teacher appointed to be their class teacher for this period was a man, although the majority of children between seven and eleven in Great Britain are taught by women. This will explain why, in this book, although teachers in general are spoken of as feminine, the class teacher of these children is referred to as masculine.

The school the children attended was in an old building with a concrete playground and no special facilities or equipment which would not normally be found in any primary school. The class was part of the school and, like any other class, shared in the general activities such as assemblies, Christmas plays, games and excursions. In the course of time, some of the children became prefects and were members of school teams. Their relations with other children were generally good and when there were difficulties, they were rarely caused by suspicions of privilege, but were of the kind which commonly occur from time to time between children in any school.

From the beginning of the second year, the children's curriculum was enriched by the introduction of German as a second language. For this subject and for music, specialist teachers were appointed and science was taught by a member of the staff of the university. In all other subjects, the children were taught by their class teacher. The educational psychologist for the project was a frequent visitor and, when not testing, would take part in whatever the children were doing. Outside visitors were discouraged and very few exceptions were made throughout the period, as we were anxious to establish and maintain the utmost normality possible in the circumstances. This was all the more important because of the unusual features such as the ability, and size of the class, although small remedial classes for slow learners existed from time to time in the school we used. Although the children's home backgrounds were not in any way uncommon, we had the advantage of the full support and continuing interest of their parents in all that was done and developed a close and friendly relationship with them.

The idea behind the project was that the experience of observing and teaching a group of clever children for four years in a primary school would furnish suggestions for the enrichment of the curriculum and examples of methods of work and general attitudes which would be helpful to teachers who have one or two children of this ability in their classes and to those who are preparing to teach. This purpose of providing something interesting and useful to teachers was our sole reason for establishing and teaching our class. The size of the class was restricted to fifteen to make adequate individual study possible, without incurring the social disadvantages of too small a group, but circumstances beyond our control prevented us from achieving a satisfactory balance in numbers between boys and girls; five girls were too few. We made no assumptions about the desirability or undesirability of segregating clever children for teaching purposes and the study was not designed to furnish any information on this question and it can not be taken as doing so. It has nothing to contribute to the vexed question of ability grouping, or to the arguments for or against small classes. These are matters on which information must be sought elsewhere.

For the sake of the children concerned, care has been taken throughout this book to avoid giving clues which might enable individuals to be identified when different aspects of personality, behaviour and work are discussed. For this reason, the common practice of using initials has been avoided and we are confident that even the parents of the children would find great difficulty in being quite sure that, in any particular example, the child in question was theirs.

After a preliminary chapter on the general characteristics of clever children, problems of identifying them, especially at the early age of seven, and some general comments on curriculum enrichment and teaching methods, the book goes on to deal more specifically with various learning activities. An attempt is made to divide them according to the kinds of thinking involved rather than by subject-matter or topic. Thus, chapter 3 is concerned with experimental enquiry and the accuracy in observing and selecting data necessary for it, while chapter 4 deals with logical reasoning. No one would pretend that this division is clear cut; it is more truly a difference of emphasis, but it seems a useful one to make when considering the children's work. Chapter 5 is devoted to imaginative work in language, art and craft and music, and is followed by one covering other activities which do not readily fall under any one of these headings. Finally, there is a short chapter listing books on various aspects of giftedness which might be helpful to a reader interested in exploring the field.

Examples of the tasks set for the children are given in some detail, not because we regard them as models of what should be done, but because we hope that they will save the time of a busy teacher who might find it quicker and easier to modify and improve them than to work out her own ideas from the beginning. This is likely to be particularly true of devising problems for young children in logical thinking which are not mainly mathematical, or at least which will not appear as such to the children. Although difficult to devise, problems of this kind are stimulating and valuable to clever children and a teacher's time is well spent in building up a stock of them. In our opinion, the best material for enriching the programme for clever children is likely to be that devised by an experienced and acutely observing teacher for those she teaches. No matter how detailed the description of our children's work may be, it aims only to provide records of experience and suggestions on which a teacher will build. It is probable, too, that although concerned with clever children of seven to eleven, much of what is said and the kinds of activities and material described would be found useful for older children of normal intelligence.

Although the needs of clever children in the early school years are gaining increasing attention, much remains to be done before we can be satisfied that their needs, as well as those of other children, are being met. More work needs to be done on the problems of recognizing their abilities at an early age and on the influence of social and economic background on the problem of recognition. Further study is needed, too, on such matters as acceleration and enrichment and on what enrichment means and how it can best be secured. These are only some of the topics which suggest themselves; others, such as that of children with high divergent thinking and spatial ability, will be indicated in the course of the following chapters.

Problems of recognition and adaptation

2

General difficulties of recognition

'What is a gifted child?' is a question easy to ask but difficult to answer. Many people think of child prodigies like the young Mozart or Karl Friedrich Gauss or they think of outstanding men and women of genius and assume that they must have been just as outstanding in their early schooldays. All would agree that such people were 'gifted', but few teachers would be so restrictive in their use of the adjective. Very few teachers have a young Mozart or Gauss in their classrooms in the whole of forty years' teaching, but many will say that they have gifted pupils. It is also unsafe to assume that the outstanding adult would necessarily have been an outstanding pupil at school.

For many people, the term 'gifted' used for children brings to mind exceptional ability in some skill such as playing a musical instrument, drawing, painting, dancing, gymnastics or sport. Such an exceptional ability is, usually, easily recognized, but difficulties occur when the adjective is used as an alternative for 'bright', 'intelligent', 'quick' or 'clever' in a general way. Used in this sense, the term 'gifted' might describe a child who is consistently at the top of his class in school work, or one who can do work normally done by children, say, two or more years older, or one who is quick in response. Legitimate as its use might be in all these examples, the term 'gifted' does not convey any precise meaning to others. A child, for example, might be quick in response with one teacher and not with another and teachers might differ in their assessment of quickness of response. There is, after all, much truth in the saying 'One man's geese are another man's swans' when it is applied to schools. Some writers have attempted to draw up lists of characteristics of 'gifted' children. These lists are often long and, as there are exceptions to each characteristic, the longer the list grows, the more imprecise it becomes. To say, for example, that a characteristic of a gifted seven-year-old is curiosity tells us little because normal children of that age brought up in a favourable environment are curious. Moreover, there are gifted children who do not appear to be particularly curious because they have been brought up in surroundings in which curiosity is not approved and they, therefore, take pains to hide it. Other characteristics and abilities may be concealed if children find they are not acceptable to those whose approval they value. Writing of American primary school children, Ruth Martinson (1968, p. 9) says:

> Occasionally a child may range four or more years beyond his grade level in measured achievement, yet give no indication of this. Since the child loves school, and is eager to adapt himself to the new environment and to please his teacher, he actually may work hard to obscure any interests and abilities which are at variance with the classroom procedures.

Appearances matter, though they may be deceptive. A child who looks bright, cheerful and tidy and whose behaviour pleases the teacher is more likely to be thought of as clever than is the child who is naughty and unco-operative or careless and untidy. The latter is a nuisance and it is only natural that his teacher should tend to overlook ability so unattractively presented. The pleasing personality of the former, on the other hand, leads his teacher to believe that he is more able than he is. For many children, especially as they grow older, the opinions of their companions are even more important than those of their teacher. Even young children do not like to be thought odd and the clever child soon learns to conceal abilities which make him laughed at or even disliked by other members of his class. If he has an ability which meets with approval, he will display it and in this way a clever boy might easily become known as a good footballer and, at the same time, maintain a reputation of being no more than an average performer at his school work. A clever child has the ability to assess a situation and whether, or how, his cleverness appears may depend to an important extent on this assessment.

Home background, too, is important to the recognition of giftedness. A clever child whose home circumstances have favoured the exercise and development of talents he needs at school is much more likely to be recognized as clever by his teacher than is the child whose home circumstances have not been so favourable. Especial care, then, is needed if clever children are to be identified in a school serving a deprived community.

Measurement

From all this it will be seen that it is by no means an easy task to pick out the gifted child or children in a class. In an enquiry conducted by Pegnato and Birch (1966, p. 78) in the junior division of a junior-senior high school in Pittsburgh, Pennsylvania, only forty-one out of ninety-one children with IQ 136 or more (Binet) were nominated by their teachers as gifted. 'Not only were more than half of the gifted missed, but a breakdown of those children referred to as gifted by the teachers revealed that almost a third (31·4 per cent) of those chosen by the teachers were *not in the gifted or superior* range but in the *average* intelligence range on the Binet.' In addition, they found that 'perhaps more than one out of 10 gifted children (10·8 per cent in this study) is achieving markedly below an optimum level.' Our experience in selecting children for the study on which this book is based was similar. Out of seventy-two children in the last term of the infant school nominated by their teachers as gifted, only twenty-four had IQs of 127 or above on the group test used (Young, 1966). Of the remaining forty-eight, nine were not tested by the Young test, and there were thus thirty-nine with IQs below 127. Seven of these had IQs below 110 and one 'gifted' child had IQ 84. Finally, of the top thirty children selected after further individual testing, fourteen, or about 50 per cent, had been nominated by their teachers. It must be remembered that the children were only in the last term in the infant school, aged about seven, and much younger than those in the Pegnato and Birch enquiry. Identifying the gifted among them was, therefore, more difficult. Nevertheless, it is surprising that two children whose reading age, as measured by the Schonell Word Recognition Test, was six years above their chronological age were not nominated by their teachers as gifted.

Aware of the imprecise meaning of the term 'gifted' in the sense of intelligent, bright, clever or quick in a general way, enquirers have usually defined it in terms of IQ as measured by standardized tests and have taken different lower limits for its use. Some have used the term for pupils of IQ 110 and above, whereas others have set their lower limit at IQ 140. The 'low' for the children on whose work this book is based was IQ 130 as measured by the Wechsler Intelligence Scale for Children (WISC). Although they are the only tried and tested measure we have, standardized tests of intelligence are by no means infallible in identifying 'gifted' children. Sometimes such children may see ambiguities in a question which are not seen by other children or, presumably, by the designer of the question. A child may, for example, refuse to fill in a blank in a sentence on the ground that the sentence could make sense as it stood and his score suffers for his acuteness or his imagination. In identifying children for this study, we supplemented the standardized test of intelligence (WISC) and the word recognition test by some items to test divergent thinking (or 'creativity' as it is sometimes called). Thus, in the group of fifteen whom we taught throughout the four years of their junior school course (ages 7+ to 11+), there were some with IQ about 130 and high divergent thinking, some with high IQ (140+) and lower divergent thinking and others not particularly low or high in either.

Need for special provision

Children of this ability may be expected to form about 2 per cent of their age group and will be regularly encountered by teachers of juniors, not necessarily as one in a class of forty each year, but never, in normal circumstances, as more than a very small minority in a class. They are the counterpart at one extreme of the slow learners at the other. In the normal classroom where the material, pace and general expectation of learning are, understandably, related to the majority, the minority at the two extremes will need special help, but it is not always realized that this is true not only of the slow learner at one end but also of the quick one at the other. A well-known American research worker (Hollingworth, 1942, p. 299) wrote: 'In the ordinary elementary school situation children of 140 IQ waste half their time. Those above 170 IQ waste practically all of their time.' It is, of course, well known that comments made in the context of the schools of one country are very rarely completely true in the context of those of another and there are those who would assert that the primary schools in Great Britain have already found the secret of providing adequately for individual differences, no matter how many pupils there are in a class. On the other hand, many parents and teachers of gifted children in this country have evidence that there is a good deal of truth in Leta Hollingworth's rather startling remarks. Many teachers, too, while approving whole-heartedly of the special consideration given to the backward children at one end of the scale, believe that more could and should be done for the highly intelligent at the other. To do so would not be to increase privilege but to do justice and to extend individual consideration to the able as well as to the other pupils in a class. In so far as his individual needs are not provided for, the gifted child can be thought of as a handicapped child and it is not unusual to find him classified in America with handicapped children, in the usual sense of the term, under the general title of 'exceptional children'. 'The real issue,' wrote Gold (1965, p. 5), 'in education of the gifted, as in education of children with moderate and low intellectual ability, is individualization in content, materials and method.'

It is sometimes urged that there is no need to make any special provision for the gifted pupils in a class. They will do well, anyway, it is said, and the teacher should concentrate her attention on those at the other end of the scale who find difficulty with their work. It is true that many gifted children will do well, if doing well means being among the top four or five in achievement in class. But is it satisfactory that a ten-year-old child with IQ 140, who is able to operate at the intellectual level of a fourteen-year-old, should be doing very well the kind of work normally done by children of his age? Children soon learn to meet expectations and if a gifted child can easily and quickly do what is required of him and, in so doing, gain the approval of teacher and parents, why should he do more? If he finds the task given him easy to accomplish, he may well become bored and his parents may have difficulty in sending him to school. Alternatively, having completed his work quickly and easily, he may look around for more challenging problems and become a ringleader in all sorts of mischievous exploits. These activities will demand special attention; perhaps more than would have been needed in the first place to provide him with challenging material, to say nothing of the disruption they may cause in the rest of the class.

Assuming, then, that it is desirable to provide materials and activities to challenge the two or three gifted children in a junior school class, the teacher may well ask what kind of attitudes and characteristics these children might show. She may already know the IQs of her children, as measured in a group test, when they

B

come from the infant school, but the test is quite likely to have missed a number of gifted and may have overestimated others. Confirmation by individual testing, of those at the top end of the scale, is, therefore, necessary, but the teacher may still look out for others whose abilities should be investigated. The difficulty is that some children's cleverness is easily apparent while others of much greater potential may not, at first sight, appear exceptionally able. This may well occur with the child whose spatial performance ability is much higher than his verbal ability, as his talents tend to be hidden in the normal educational setting which puts a premium on verbal ability. The same is often true of the highly imaginative, divergent thinker who is not a ready or able verbalizer. Such children are easily overlooked and their talents wasted in any unsympathetic system. It is worth bearing in mind in this connection that some of the children with high spatial performance ability could be potential scientists or engineers and they are, generally speaking more likely to be boys than girls. Thus, there is a very real danger that clever boys, with the kinds of talents particularly needed in an industrial society, are going unrecognized and their development is being stunted because suitable provision for it is not made. Making suitable provision presents peculiar difficulties in an educational system mainly directed towards the development of verbal skills and measuring success by them. More attention should be given to recognizing and fostering exceptional spatial and divergent thinking abilities in school from an early age.

It is clear that a superficial observation of the activities and reactions of children in the classroom can be misleading and, for reasonable success in recognizing the gifted, a teacher needs considerable experience of children of the age group and much practice in observing and analysing their behaviour. Many of the behaviour characteristics which are fairly evident in gifted students are barely observable when the children first come to the junior school at seven. It has always to be remembered, as Bridges insists in his account of the Brentwood experiment (1969), that gifted children are children and not miniature adults and it is not at all unlikely that a gifted seven-year-old will want to be near his teacher as much as any other child in the class and will have the same desire for affection and approval. If, after careful observation, a teacher suspects that one of her children may be gifted and wishes to make sure his abilities are challenged, she should refer him to an educational psychologist for individual testing. She should not hold back for fear of being mistaken because, generally speaking, it is better to refer too many in this way than too few if the latter course runs the risk of leaving individual abilities undiscovered.

Signs of ability

When the teacher of seven-year-old children faces her new class at the beginning of the year, she is likely to notice any child who is an exceptionally good reader. The child reads a lot and can read aloud well. Many gifted children will show this characteristic and it is easy to recognize and to look for, but it should be remembered that its emergence will depend a good deal on the child's background and his reaction to the material provided in the classroom. Nevertheless, it seems unlikely that a gifted child, brought up in normal circumstances, will not be able to read as well as the average child of his age and it is probable that he will do very much better than that, or will soon do so, given the interest of suitable material. Some gifted children read very well, showing ability to understand far beyond the normal for their age, but are not interested in fiction. They use their ability as a tool for other purposes. For example, a child might turn easily to works of reference like encyclopaedias for information to help him solve a problem he has encountered in model-making. It is not uncommon to find a seven-year-old child doing this who shows no interest in reading as a general activity. Such a child, although gifted, may need a good deal of persuasion before he will try anything outside the range of his immediate interests. He reads little, but very selectively. There are, on the other hand, clever children who, although they read a lot and like reading, read little else but comics because the only books around them are too childish. Every teacher knows that to generalize about children is always hazardous, and, perhaps, never more hazardous than about the highly intelligent; yet reading ability which appears exceptional in quality or quantity to the experienced teacher of seven-year-olds should lead her to look for other signs that the child might be gifted.

One of these signs might be an unusual ability to deal with abstract problems, 'to work things out in his head', as we say. A bright seven-year-old might, for example, show this in being able to play a well-thought-out game of chess, or in arriving at the answer to a problem in arithmetic with a minimum number of steps. When given a manipulative puzzle to do, he might be seen to consider the most likely method of attack, whereas other children would begin at once and proceed solely by trial and error. The teacher may also find that he is not satisfied when he has done the puzzle; he wants to find out whether there are other ways of doing it.

Curiosity, wanting to find out, is, of course, a common characteristic of young children and is closely related, in its strength, to their environment. It is seen in their constant questioning, both at home and in school, if the environment is stimulating and classroom relationships relaxed. Parents and teachers of pre-school and very young children know, however, that questions are not always prompted by curiosity, but may be asked in order to attract the adult's attention. These are not genuine questions in the sense that the child is curious to know the answers and careful observation may show that the persistent questioner in class is not as intellectually curious as he seems. No matter how genuine a child's questions may be, the experienced teacher will not be impressed merely by their number. It is their quality, the unusual perceptiveness or thoughtfulness which prompts them which is a more reliable clue to the child's intellectual ability. One difficulty is that some questions, though good ones genuinely stimulated by what the teacher is doing, may be far removed from the theme the teacher wishes the class to pursue. It is, to say the least, disconcerting if, in a lesson on the ancient Egyptians a film strip is being shown and a child suddenly asks: 'How do you get a square picture out of a round lens?' The question, from a seven-year-old, is a good one and contains considerable opportunities of educational value but at the time it is merely a nuisance. The problem it presents is how to postpone the question for discussion at a more suitable time without discouraging the child or making him feel that he was at fault in asking. Although not relevant to the topic, the question is relevant to the situation and may indicate a capacity for divergent thinking which is worth fostering.

Quickness of response is also common in clever children. If the teacher asks a question, a clever child will often call out the answer almost before she has finished asking it and long before most of the other children in the class have made any response. With a group of clever seven-year-olds this makes any kind of discussion impossible and in a class of mixed abilities it removes the opportunity for the other children to learn by puzzling out the answer for themselves.

If, for example, to demonstrate a principle of floating, a teacher weighs a boat, places it in water and it floats, then weighs a nail which is much lighter than the boat, places it in water and it sinks, and a child calls out: 'If you hammered it flat, it would float', the teacher hardly welcomes the interruption, especially if hammering the nail flat is the next thing she was going to do. In this incident the seven-year-old gave the solution to the problem before the teacher had finished posing it; he did not even wait for a question to be asked. Behaviour of this kind is a welcome sign of giftedness but, like the apparently irrelevant, but genuine, question, it presents the teacher with a problem. Instead of having to encourage the child to respond as she has to do with so many others in her class, she has to find some way of restraining him sufficiently to give the others a chance without, at the same time, fostering in him a growing feeling of frustration. Again it must be emphasized that, as with the other signs so far discussed, eagerness to respond is not a necessary characteristic of a gifted child. Such a child may be shut up tightly like a clam, and the teacher may find it difficult to get anything out of him. When, however, he does respond, the teacher will often be surprised by the quality of thought or perception which the response indicates.

The ability to work quickly is another characteristic shown by many gifted children. If their class is set a series of problems in mathematics, they finish before anyone else and, unless specially provided for, will turn their attention to other, perhaps disruptive, activities. These quick workers are not, however, necessarily accurate: a child may solve the problem quickly but get his answer wrong because he has made some silly mistake in computation. It is not unusual for a clever child to invent mathematically-sound short cuts to spare himself tedious calculation and yet get a wrong answer because his attention has been distracted or because he has lost interest. He may be quick and inventive in problem solving but inaccurate in repetitive or mechanical computation out of sheer boredom. On the other hand, there are some gifted children with such a passion for accuracy that they are afraid to suggest or to take any step until they are quite sure it is the correct one. Such a child may appear to be so slow that the teacher is tempted to regard him as dull or lethargic and anything but clever. The problem is to distinguish between slowness of working arising from anxiety and perfectionism and that arising from sheer laziness or lack of ability, because any attempt to drive the anxious perfectionist may only make matters worse as it is encouragement that is needed.

Every teacher knows that the popular idea of the clever child as a withdrawn, physically puny, anti-social bookworm is completely and utterly mistaken. Generally speaking, he is more likely to be physically as well as mentally superior, interested in the hobbies and pastimes of his age group, socially acceptable and a leader in his group. A series of tests, referred to in a later chapter, showed that our children had greater ability than usual in dynamic activities involving basic physical qualities such as strength and speed. There are, of course, exceptions; there are clever children who are withdrawn and physically inferior to their companions but investigators are generally agreed that they are unusual.

A characteristic noticed by many observers and one that came to our attention early is that quite young gifted children are usually happy to work on their own, each at his own speed. If they are interested, they become absorbed in what they are doing and dislike being in any way distracted. In these circumstances, there seems to be no reason why they should not be encouraged to work individually and the teacher who has one or two of these children in a class of forty can give them interesting and challenging tasks for individual accomplishment without feeling that she should be making them spend the time on group enterprises. Teaching machines may be helpful here but special programmes are needed, as normal ones for the age group are often unsuitable. A clever child who is good at arithmetic, using a linear programme designed for his age group, may reach the final answer when he is only half-way through the questions on the programme. He does not need to work through each step but leaps ahead and is frustrated by careful plodding. It would be foolish to expect him to restrict his pace to that of the programme; if he is quick enough to see and take short cuts to a solution, he should be encouraged to do so. Interest is the key to absorption for these children as it is for others and, for them, interest must involve challenge. They are bored by tasks they find too easy. On the other hand, they are capable of becoming completely absorbed in an activity and of remaining absorbed much longer than the teacher would normally expect. For this to occur, a child's initial interest must be supported by a conviction that the activity is worthwhile, otherwise it will soon be lost and the child will quickly turn his attention to something else. Once committed, however, a clever child can and will often surprise his teacher by his capacity for perseverance towards an end which to him is challenging and valuable.

Children's interests depend very much on their backgrounds and this is true of clever as well as of other children. It is not, however, unusual to find that a clever child is more selective in his interests than are most seven- or eight-year-olds. His preferences are often strongly marked and matched by variation in performance. One child may, for example, enjoy mathematical and other problems requiring logical reasoning for their solution but at the same time be an unwilling reader and lack freedom in expressing himself in speech or writing. Another child, by his interest in practical problems and his manipulative skill, may seem, even at this early age, to have the makings of an engineer, while yet another one may be a voracious reader and happy in imaginative writing in prose or verse. This child, outstanding in imaginative writing, may be no more competent in mathematics than the average for his age. The teacher, then, should not expect the gifted child in her class to be outstanding in everything her pupils do.

Although happy to work individually, gifted children, even at seven, are often highly competitive. Being very intelligent, they know that they are so and they like being the best performers and may even become almost obsessive about it. 'Obsessive' must not, however, be taken to mean openly conceited. No one likes a boaster and a clever child in an ordinary class soon learns to play down his achievements with his companions. If, on the other hand, a seven-year-old of IQ around 140 or more finds himself for the first time in a group with others of the same ability the experience can be very upsetting for him. After being the most able in a group of children of his own age, it is shattering for him to learn that there are so many as good as, perhaps even better than, he is, although the lesson may be a valuable one in humility. One or two of our children, for example, were sure when they first came to the class that they were not as clever as the others. Fortunately, their interest and motivation, generally strong in able children, overcame any temptation to give up and helped them to adjust successfully to their new situation.

A brief reference has already been made to the mistaken view that clever children are usually 'odd' and socially withdrawn. If they are, the explanation is often to be sought elsewhere; their cleverness is not necessarily responsible. Parental expectations, which may or may not be related to a child's intellectual ability, and the emotional climate of the home are of crucial importance, especially if the child is particularly sensitive. The children in our group, with perhaps one or two exceptions, were generally well adjusted and showed higher than normal extroversion when tested in their first year. Statements of this kind, however, about children as young as seven to eight have to be made and received with caution as they may be reflecting conditions which are purely temporary but happen to obtain when the tests are made. The views of parents and teachers are longer term but are often difficult to interpret and assess. The following are examples of these views:

'A very happy child; confident and untroubled; fits in anywhere; keen to express opinions.' 'Head and shoulders above the others in his class; inventive in making things; to some teachers pleasant and likeable, to others aggressive and naughty.'

'Not shy but confident and forward; always in too much of a hurry; untidy; would drive you mad with questions; sulks or makes scences if thwarted.' 'Showed initiative and ability to organize; very quick orally; quick grasp.'

'Lacks confidence; sure she is not as clever as others in her group; slow to make friends; needs and likes routine; timid but gets on quite well with other children; worries a lot.' 'Obviously clever but lacks personality; mother over-anxious for her progress; needs constant re-assurance; a perfectionist; rather withdrawn.'

'Thoughtful and affectionate; helpful to others; makes friends easily; dislikes being on his own.' 'Very well integrated personality; sets very high standards for himself; does not like to let himself down; his work very neat and well organized; an excellent member of class in every way.'

'Very highly strung with sharp temper but very jolly and usually good-natured; affectionate; not many friends of own age; with adults a lot.' 'Happy, eager and attractive; would interfere with and boss other children and needed a firm hand.'

'Strong sense of humour becoming keener all the time; friendly; confident, with a mind of his own; happy; not demonstrative.' 'Did not appear clever; quiet; difficult to interest.'

'Quiet; confident; selective in friendships; tends to be critical of other children; nervous at times.' 'Rather volatile; not always controlled; sometimes unreasonable and inconsistent.'

'Can be extremely stubborn; can be led but not driven; gets on well with others; easily worried, particularly about school work; always wanting reasons for things; very lively interest.' 'Stolid; did not appear particularly intelligent in infant school; quiet; thoughtful; occasionally surprised teacher with unusual comments.'

In each of these extracts the first set of comments is by the parents and the second by the teacher of the child in the infant school. All the children were of IQ 130 or above, but there are few clues to this in the comments. Most of them would be appropriate to children of a very wide range of ability. At the same time, there is nothing to suggest noticeable 'oddness' in personality. In one or two instances, it will be suspected that a child presented a different face in school from the one he showed at home and it is possible to pick out children likely and unlikely to fit easily into the educational system. Although generally independent and confident for their age these children need the emotional support of a sympathetic classroom background if their abilities are to flourish.

Adaptation of curriculum

It is clear, from the characteristics so far discussed, that the presence of one or two children of the intellectual ability indicated by IQ 130 and upwards in a class of, say, forty is likely to set a problem for the class teacher. In the following chapters various aspects of the curriculum for seven- to eleven-year-olds and its enrichment are discussed and examples of some of the material and activities enjoyed by the children in our group are given. 'The task in education of gifted children,' writes Gold (1965, p. 143) 'is not simply to add more reading, more arithmetic, more science, but to help the bright child to find greater meaning in the life about him.' His target should be better quality rather than greater quantity, depth as well as breadth. Ruth Martinson (1968, pp. 3–4) is right to remind us that:

Much of our error in dealing with the upper reaches of human potential lies in qualitative under-estimation. Most of the frustrations which are expressed about unreasonable demands upon the child are reactions to excessive *quantity* of requirements, and toward inappropriate content. Rarely if ever are criticisms directed toward overestimated *quality* of content. The problem is compounded because the individual who is subjected to *repetitous* content is the very one who learns easily with less repetition than the average person.

If, for example, a bright child can do quickly and accurately the sums his classmates find difficult, there is no point in requiring him to do more of the same kind in order to keep him occupied. To do so will only invite boredom and frustration. He should be moving on to more difficult concepts and operations.

Any programme planned for gifted children should aim at (a) intellectual challenge through the quality rather than the quantity of the work; (b) developing self-direction and independence of thought and action; (c) encouraging originality and imagination. In discussing the programme, many writers use the terms 'enrichment' and 'acceleration' and attempt to distinguish between them. The former may denote a widening of the whole curriculum by the provision of additional activities or the inclusion of an additional subject or subjects, perhaps a foreign language for the abler eight-year-olds. It may also denote exploration at greater depth within the scope of the curriculum for the age group. This is particularly suitable for highly intelligent children with their ability to lose themselves in a project and to remain occupied by it over long periods of time. Acceleration, on the other hand, is used to describe the situation in which the bright child in a particular age group is set to do work normally considered suitable for older children. Although, at first sight, this distinction between acceleration and enrichment may seem plain enough, it is not so in practice and the adoption of one rather than the other for clever children very often proves impossible. The early stages of mathematics, for example, are progressive in the sense that the child must master one set of concepts and operations before he can proceed to the next. Having mastered one set, he is ready to move on, and it is enrichment for him if his programme allows him to do so. Thus, for the seven- to eleven-year-old child who is clever at mathematics, acceleration and enrichment in this part of his programme will be inseparable. That this may lead to difficulties for him at a later stage is not an argu-

ment for holding him back but rather for challenging material to be
provided for him throughout his school career.

One of the problems is to find the right balance between prescrip-
tion and freedom in providing materials for the gifted in a class.
As we have seen, these children are likely to be showing independence of thought and action by the time they reach the ages to which
this book relates, and many of them long before then. It is not, for
example, unusual to find a clever child self-sufficient for his age
even at three. If this independence and capacity for self-direction is
to be developed, it will not be done by the over-prescription and
detailed direction of activities by the teacher. Such direction will be
particularly frustrating to the divergent thinker, the 'creative' child
(Spaulding, 1968, p. 233).

> The 'creative intellectual', or creatively gifted appears most
> highly motivated and constructively occupied in settings where
> limits are clearly set but which permit a wide range of choice
> for self-direction. The creative or inventive thinker appears not
> so much to want to become less involved with the classroom
> activity but to be permitted to enter into each with a greater
> degree of autonomy and responsibility. The 'conforming
> achiever' seems most at ease and most productive when the lines
> of expectation are closely drawn and instructions clearly given.

At the same time, young children seem to find reassurance in knowing what is expected of them, and those who are gifted are no
exception. While avoiding too detailed direction, therefore, the
teacher will need to map the route sufficiently for the child to get his
bearings and recognize the path he is following. It is, for example,
possible to present a child with a problem which needs certain
information for its solution without telling him what it is or where
to find it. The teacher can still help the child, if he wants help, to
find the information he thinks is needed, without commenting on
whether it is relevant or not. He will find it interesting and in-
structive to watch how the child tackles the problem and to see what
information he chooses as relevant and why he chooses it. In
realizing the importance of defining and understanding the problem,
the child exercises clear thinking and uses his imagination in deciding
what information is needed to solve it.

The clever child between seven and eleven is, thus, likely to
flourish in a classroom where he is free from over-insistent pressures

to conform to a narrowly defined pattern; a classroom where originality of thought and expression is encouraged and where there is
plenty of opportunity for him to work on his own with challenging
material. Opportunity should also be given him to learn to examine
and criticize his own thinking and that of others. For this purpose,
as well as for fertility of ideas, a wide background of information is
needed and the provision and development of such a background is
an obvious and easy objective of the curriculum for the gifted.
Plenty of books covering a wide range of topics should be available;
some which the child will read through, others which he will learn to
consult for information. A child cannot learn to weigh the value of
his own ideas unless he has ideas to examine and the teacher must
find a way of encouraging this critical examination without inhibiting
the flow of ideas. Some writers advocate deliberate attempts to
stimulate the production of ideas by specific exercises emphasizing
the number of ideas produced in a given time, regardless of their
absurdity. For example, the children might be asked to list the
names of all the objects they can think of which have certain given
qualities, or the different uses they can think of for a given object
other than its usual one; the more suggestions a child makes within
the time set, the better his performance. The results of such a short
'brain-storming' session, as it is sometimes called, can later be
subjected to critical examination by the children. The divergent
thinker among clever children may show surprising ability at guess-
ing the solution to a problem because he is able to see it in an
unusual frame of reference which would not occur to a more conventional thinker. Such a child should be encouraged to use his
'contrary imagination' even though many of his guesses prove
mistaken. He will soon see where he has gone wrong and will be
anxious to try again. In general, however, the problem posed by the
antipathy between the production and evaluation of ideas, like so
many other problems, can only be solved by the teacher in the light
of her knowledge of the particular child. Her carefully considered
experience will show her the degree of encouragement and its
direction desirable in each situation.

The clever child must not, of course, be looked on simply as a
problem-solver; material giving scope for his imagination must be
provided for him as for any other child. Art and music, dramatic
work, story-telling and reading all have their contribution to make
here. Given an initial suggestion and the opportunity for free

writing, these children will often surprise their teachers with the ambitiousness, length and originality of their stories. Later chapters will describe in more detail the activities of the young children we taught in these and other parts of their programme. The teacher with one or two such children in a large class will not be able to devise a programme for them completely different from that for the rest of the class but she can make it more challenging and can take steps to provide suitable conditions. These have been discussed above and are well summarized by Ruth Martinson (1968, p. 55):

> The teacher . . . must take cognizance of the fact that gifted children function better in an environment where they have time to seek answers to broad, major questions rather than to finite, detailed questions; where they can plan their own ways to find the best answers; where they can discuss implications and formulate generalizations about the meanings of the answers; where they can learn about the unusual and new, or develop new ideas of their own for reaction; where they can use library and community resources without imposed limits; where their right to question, enquire, and create is nurtured and encouraged, and where they are given opportunity to work as deeply, as independently, and for as long a time as they need to, in order to attain satisfactory closure for themselves.

The teacher

The question is sometimes asked: 'Is it necessary for a teacher to have as high an IQ rating as that of the gifted children in her class?' The answer, at least for teachers of children up to the age of eleven, is no. A teacher's fears on this account are groundless, provided she is prepared to realize and accept her strengths and weaknesses. It has already been emphasized that gifted children are still children and have the limited experience of children. There is no need for the teacher to pretend to knowledge or ability she does not possess. Indeed, it is dangerous to do so with these children, as they are quick to discover pretence of this kind. They soon find that there are many things, regarded by them as important, which their teacher knows more about or can do better than they and they are ready to admire her for it. Ability to draw on the blackboard or to play some games or to make models better than they can will often establish their teacher's reputation for them overnight. They are, however, demanding to teach and the teacher will find it necessary to read widely and to keep her knowledge constantly renewed. She should be attentive to and sympathetic towards the needs of gifted children as of any other children in her class. She needs to be a close and reflective observer of children if she is to discover the gifted in her class and, having discovered them, to see the directions of their giftedness in order to provide the right kind of challenge for them. At times, as we have seen, she will need all her patience to bear with the non-conformers among them. Like all exceptional children, they present a challenge to the teacher but one which is well worth meeting and rewarding in the satisfaction it can bring.

Observation and enquiry

3

Every teacher knows that it is impossible to make clear-cut divisions among the activities of children in school. Observation and enquiry, for example, which are the concern of this chapter make use of logical reasoning and imagination which are the subjects of later ones. Divisions have to be made, however, for the sake of clarity and so long as they are not taken to imply that a child is active in only one direction at a time, no great harm is done. In this chapter we are concerned with that part of our children's curriculum which provides for the systematic gathering of information from books and for experimental enquiry involving the collection, examination and classification of data and the formulation and testing of hypotheses.

Finding information

Bright children are often quick to observe and notice details which may escape the attention of others. If a child shows a capacity in this direction, it is worth encouraging as it is a necessary basis for any efficient enquiry. It is, of course, the foundation of experimental work in science, which is the subject of a later section in this chapter, and it can also be usefully directed towards the efficient use of books as sources of information. One way of doing this is by devising a series of cards referring to books available in the class or school library which the children can work through individually. Our children found this activity interesting and enjoyable even as early as their first year in the class when they were between seven and eight years old. We aimed to accustom them to using books efficiently for information by consulting tables of contents and indexes and to reporting their findings clearly and simply. At the same time, we hoped to widen their horizons by introducing them to a diversity of subjects, thereby not only increasing their general knowledge but also suggesting possible new interests to them.

Finding out work cards

We devised some sixty cards which our children began to use in their second term in the class, that is at about eight years old. The first forty cards were graded to present work of increasing complexity to match the child's growing skill and were related to books published by A. and C. Black, mainly in their Junior Reference Series, which were available in the class library. We used these books because they present information on a wide range of topics in a straightforward way, with clearly drawn diagrams and illustrations, and a good index in each book. In addition, we thought they were likely to be widely found in school libraries.

The following examples from the cards are given to show the kind of questions asked and to indicate their increasing difficulty. It is a simple matter for any teacher to devise cards related to the suitable books available and she is likely to find, as we did, that eventually some children will want to make up cards to add to the series for their companions to do. This, of course, only comes later when a child has acquired some skill and feels confident about finding information and being able to express it clearly and concisely.

The basic layout of the first forty of our cards was the same, but in the early ones the child was simply required to answer various specific questions by finding the correct information in a designated chapter and putting it into a sentence, as in this example:

Finding out   *Card 1*

Most books that we use for finding information have a table of contents and an index.
The table of contents is usually at the beginning of the book and it tells us what each chapter is about and the page on which it begins.
The index, which is at the back of the book, tells us on which pages we shall find information about the people, places and things mentioned in the book.
Find the book *Stars and Space*. Use the table of contents to find the chapter on the moon.
Read the chapter. Now answer these questions:

1 What is the title of the chapter?
2 Why do you think the author calls the moon our companion?
3 How long does it take the moon to revolve round the earth?
4 On photographs of the moon we find things that look like holes. What are these holes called?
5 We can also find patches on the moon's surface. What are these called?
6 Is there water on the moon?
7 The temperature on the moon at midday would be . . .?
8 The temperature on the moon at midnight would be . . .?
9 Write down any interesting facts you have discovered about the moon.

The other cards of the first ten were similar:

Finding out   *Card 7*

Find the book *Looking at Life* by Elsie Proctor.
It is Book 4 in the series *Looking at Nature*.
Use the table of contents to find the chapter called 'Protecting Wild Life'. Read the chapter.
Now answer these questions:
1 Why do we need to protect wild life?
2 What is the name of the national society which protects wild life?
3 Name four nature reserves.
4 Name the rare bird that has been saved.
5 Look up 'Protection of Wild Life in Africa'.
  Name a famous national park in South Africa.
6 What is a rondavel?
7 Name three animals you might find in the South African National Park.

The wording of the questions was found to be very important. It is essential to make clear what you are asking of the child and to be sure that the question framed leaves no room for ambiguity. Clever children, like all others, need to know exactly what you mean, but some of them may take a delight in misunderstanding if there is any opportunity for them to do so. A carelessly framed question will in all likelihood invite a wholly unexpected and, perhaps, unwelcome answer. When reading the children's work it is important to examine carefully any answer which seems to indicate misunderstanding be-

C

cause the question may prove to have been ambiguous and the child's answer may be fully justified and, however unwelcome, must be accepted. Unless questions are specific and carefully worded, this apparent misunderstanding may often occur with clever children.

An example of this occurred in card 1. The answer to the first question, the title of the chapter, was 'The moon, our companion in space.' The second question originally read 'Why do you think the author uses this title?' The answer was expected to show that the significance of the word 'companion' had been appreciated by making some such statement as 'Because the moon always stays close to the earth.' However, one boy, blessed with a very logical mind, gave the answer 'Because that's what it's about.' It is not unlikely that a teacher for whom the 'right' answer is the one she wants would have marked this wrong, whereas it correctly showed up the ambiguity of the question which had then to be revised. It illustrates the ever present danger that a clever child might be penalized for his originality and intelligence.

Gradually the questions on the cards were made more complex. A single sentence answer was not enough. Questions were framed in such a way that a child who was interested could write a short paragraph on certain topics. Questions 3 and 6 in the example below are of this type.

Finding out   *Card 11*

Find *The Story of the Theatre* by David Male.
Using the contents, find the chapter 'Shakespeare and the Globe'.
Read this chapter. Answer these questions with a sentence or sentences:
1 What was the name of the first theatre opened in London? When was it opened and by whom?
2 Who disapproved of the theatres?
3 What amusements were available on Bankside?
4 Draw a picture of the interior of the Globe theatre and name the parts.
5 Find the names of five plays by Shakespeare.
6 Write a short account of Shakespeare's life.

As the cards progressed, paragraphs were specifically asked for in certain questions.

Finding out   *Card 17*

Find *Looking at the World Today* which is Book 4 of the series *Looking at Geography* by Gadsby and Ashby.

Turn to the chapter on Brazil, and answer the following questions:

1 What is the great river of Brazil called? What is its length? What sort of country does it run through?
2 Can you name six valuable commodities found in the Amazon forests?
3 What can you discover about the port of Manaos?
4 Coffee is Brazil's most valuable crop. Write a paragraph about coffee growing. Draw any pictures that you think are necessary to illustrate it.
5 Draw a map of South America, showing where Brazil is. Mark on the map the course of the Amazon, and the positions of Manaos, Rio de Janeiro, Brasilia and Sao Paulo.
6 What can you discover about Brazil's industries and mineral resources?
7 What crops are grown on Brazil's coastal plain?

As the questions became more demanding (as in question 5 below) an attempt was made to guide the child's choice of material by a number of supplementary questions. The possibilities of the index were re-stated in greater detail.

Finding out   *Card 21*

Find *Travel by Road* by R. J. Unstead.

Turn to the index at the back of the book.

The index is there to help you to find information quickly about things you are interested in. It takes you directly to the page or pages you need without the trouble of reading the whole chapter, or the whole book.

1 Find the name 'Daimler' in the index. You will find it says 'Daimler, Gottlieb 58'. This means that Gottlieb Daimler is mentioned on page 58. Turn to the page and write down, in your own words, what you find about him. Then use the index to answer these questions:
2 Who was General Wade?
3 What was a whirlicote?
4 Draw a picture of a state landau.

5 Write a paragraph about the omnibus. Find out what the word omnibus means. When did the first one appear in London? What was its route and what was its fare? Tell in your own words any other interesting information which you can discover.

6 What was a curricle?

In later cards (31–40) suggestions were made for wider reading in the subject, where suitable books were known to be available. The work needed was much greater in these, and the child had to select what he considered was important from the information available.

Finding out   Card 32

Find *Stars and Space* by Patrick Moore.
You can find enough information in it for the card.
You can make your work more interesting, however, by using books on the subject which are in the school library or at home, or in the public library. The librarian will be only too willing to help you if you ask.
Wherever possible, the titles of useful books will be given in this and the following cards.

1 Write some paragraphs, in your own words, about telescopes. Make clear the precise nature of reflecting, refracting and radio telescopes. Try to find where the largest example of each type is to be found. Draw diagrams or pictures to illustrate your account (try the encyclopaedia which your school library should have).

2 Write a description of the moon. Describe its features and size. Find its distance from the earth and if it rotates. Write about man's exploration of the moon's surface. (World Books Encyclopaedia has a good article on the moon. *Planets*, published by Life Books, is very informative.)

3 Write a paragraph about each of the following planets:
   (a) Mercury
   (b) Mars
   (c) Venus
   (d) Saturn
   (e) Jupiter

4 What is:
   (a) a light year?

(b) a comet?
(c) a meteor?
(d) a meteorite?

Towards the end of the series a unified piece of work on a central theme was required. Care was taken to provide a framework for the child to work to. As many key words as possible were suggested to help him to use the index efficiently.

Finding out   *Card 37*

Find the book *Arms and Armour* by Frederick Wilkinson.
There is a second book *Arms and Armour* also by Frederick Wilkinson (Hamlyn all-colour paperbacks) which will be very useful.
Write an illustrated history of the sword starting with the bronze age and draw pictures to illustrate each type of weapon you describe. Use the index and the glossary at the back of the book.
You will show the bronze age swords. What was the khepesh? Why was iron preferred to bronze? Describe the Roman soldier's sword and how it was used. The Viking swords were quite different; there is a good picture of one in the book. To what do the terms 'pommel' and 'quillon' refer? Was the scramasax a sword? There were many types of sword used in the Middle Ages; describe the estoc, claymore and glamboyant blade. What sort of sword would a Landsknecht prefer? Write about the rapier, smallsword and sabre. When did the duel and the art of fencing come into fashion?

The subjects selected were dictated by the reference books available. In the forty initial cards twenty-one subjects were introduced, from furniture and heraldry to deep sea fishing and farming. Certain topics, such as travel on land, ships, aircraft, coal mining and sea fishing, were used several times to give the child a perspective of the essential matter in each. At a later stage, four of these topics were developed into projects which engaged the interest and effort of individual children over a considerable time.

The approach so far described may, at first sight, seem too formal but it is important that a child engaged on work which is truly individual should have the support and guidance of a structure. The framework of instructions, questions and suggestions for reference is intended as something on which the child can build, not as a strait-jacket to constrict him. The teacher will not only design cards suitable for her pupils and provide a structural support for their work but will encourage them to see it not just as an exercise but as a means of pursuing more efficiently their own interests. She will have to be on her guard to prevent the competitiveness of some of these children from turning the working of the cards into a race. Speed of completion is not the object. The children must be brought to realize that the effort, care, judgment and intelligence they bring to the task are important; and that their satisfaction will come, not from doing more cards than anyone else, but from the thorough completion of each card and from their increasing efficiency in finding information. The teacher should, therefore, ensure that a child has worked with care, obeyed the instructions, followed up every reference, and understands what he has written; but, beyond this, she should encourage the child's individuality of approach. A child will often want to do more than a card demands, and, if he is already interested in the subject, he may have more information about it than is contained in the book suggested for reference. For example, an eight-year-old boy who was exceptionally interested in space travel was able to answer all the questions on the first card in great detail without reference to a book. There was no point, therefore, in insisting that he work through the questions with reference to the book named on the card; to have done so would only have invited frustration. It was, however, quite reasonable to ask him to find confirmation for facts he gave which were not in the book, thus providing a valuable exercise in finding out and, at the same time, drawing his attention to the need to find support for his statements. Another boy in our group always took longer than expected over his work because he had an obsession for order, neatness and detail. He was very proud of his work and took great pains with it. To have been continually urging him to work more quickly would have discouraged a trait which might later develop into a scholarly habit of mind.

Sometimes an item on a card would arouse an unexpectedly strong interest in one of the children. One boy, for example, working on a musical instrument card, became interested in pipe organs. Using the *Oxford Companion to Music* as a reference, he spent hours puzzling out their construction and drawing diagrams of different types of organ. He even attempted, unsuccessfully, to make a model of a mediaeval organ, and then his interest waned. Teachers of clever children must be prepared for the emergence of unexpected interests and allow time for their pursuit, even if, as is very likely, they prove to be transitory. While they last, the child is able to enrich his experience by pursuing in depth something he sees as worth while and he should be encouraged to do so.

It is not, however, suggested that a child should work only at the cards concerned with his particular interests, that he should be allowed to pick them out and ignore the others. The knowledge that there are cards relating to an interest later in the series should encourage him to persist with earlier ones and, in doing so, he will probably find other subjects of interest which were unknown to him before. In this way, too, his experience is enriched. From time to time, one of our children would complain that a particular card, for example, one on costume, theatre or nature study, was a 'girl's card' or one on aircraft, ships or armour a 'boy's card'. It was, however, interesting that, very often, the children later volunteered the information that they were glad they had been made to work on the card because they had found it interesting, after all.

The last nineteen cards in the set were intended to provide the instructions needed to launch a child on a full-scale project. A child working on one of them would need to refer to several books, the titles of which were on his card. The help of the local public library in providing books may be necessary if similar work is attempted in a normal class, although there are many good inexpensive books on the market providing information on a wide range of suitable subjects. When a child had finished the first forty cards he was allowed to work on these more difficult ones, the first two of which were to be done by everyone. The seemingly big increase in difficulty which they present proved to be more apparent than real because of the thorough practice provided by the earlier ones. To a large extent, each child was now on his own, dealing with a much more loosely structured situation and having to select what he would write from a wider body of information. He was, however, given a simple method of working and a framework of chapter headings to guide him. In fact, the complexity of the subject is governed at this stage not so much by what the child sees in it in the way of possibilities but by the information available. The two subjects used, the theatre and submarines, were limited by the material available for reference. Thus, although an adult could find in either topic material enough for several volumes, in practice they proved to be ideal bridging subjects for the children.

Finding out   *Card 41*

The Theatre

Books which will be useful:

The Story of the Theatre, Ladybird.
The Theatre, Macdonald, Junior Reference.
The Story of the Theatre, David Male, Black.
Look at Theatres, Ivor Brown, Panther.
Look at the Circus, Noel Streatfeild, Panther.
Shakespeare's Theatre, C. Walter Hodges, Oxford.

You should read the Ladybird book right through first. Use David Male's *The Story of the Theatre* for the early chapters. If you can borrow a copy of *Shakespeare's Theatre*, it will be very useful for your chapter 3. Divide your story into the following chapters:

1 *The Greeks* Write about the plays which they watched. Describe and draw their theatres. Describe and draw the actors' costumes.
2 *The Middle Ages* Write about the strolling players, guild plays and church drama. Draw a 'pageant'.
3 *The Time of Shakespeare* Describe the Globe Theatre and draw a picture of it. Write as much as you can discover about Shakespeare. Describe the scenery and costume used.
4 *The Theatre in King Charles' Time* Describe the theatre buildings in Restoration times, the audiences, costumes and plays.
5 *The Eighteenth Century* Discover as much as you can about players and plays, costumes and scenery.
6 *Victorian Times* Describe the music halls and the English pantomime. Write about its links with commedia dell' arte and harlequinade.
7 *Modern Times* Describe how a modern theatre is lit. Write as much as you can discover about actors, plays and playwrights. Describe a television theatre.
8 *The Circus* If you can find enough information, write an account of the history of circuses and what the modern circus is like.

Finding out   *Card 42*

Submarines

These books contain information about submarines:

Look at Submarines, Edward Young, a Panther Look Book.

Warships from 1860 to the Present Day, H. T. Lenton,
Hamlyn all colour paperback.

Encyclopaedia of Ships, Enzo Angelucci, Odhams.

Submarines, E. C. Stephens, Bailey Brothers.

Submarines, Gilbert Hackfort-Jones, Frederick Muller.

Submarines, Carey Miller, Piccolo Books.

All about Submarines, G. Weller, W. H. Allen.

Ships, Time-Life Books, Life Science Library.

Inventions that Made the Modern World (the chapter
'Exploring the depths').

Any encyclopaedia which you have may be useful.
(*World Books Encyclopaedia* has a good article.)

Read *Look at Submarines* first and get a good grasp of the
subject before you do any further reading. Divide your work
into the following chapters:

1 The story of early submarines up to the early Holland boats
2 The development from early Holland boats to modern
conventional submarines
3 How a submarine works
4 The atomic submarine and modern research submarines

Draw pictures and diagrams to illustrate your account. If you
are interested in reading about the exploits of submariners and
their hunters, the following books may interest you and you
will find others in the public library.

The Battle of the Atlantic, Duncan Macintyre, Pan/Batsford
Battle Books.

Walker, R. N., Terence Robertson, Pan Books.

The Cruel Sea, Nicholas Monsarrat, Cassell, Cadet Edition.

These are stories of the British navy's fight against the U-boat:

One of our Submarines, Edward Young, Penguin.

Dardanelles Patrol, Shankland and Hunter, Mayflower.

Sunk, Mochitsura Hashimoto, Panther.

When these two cards were completed a child could choose one of a
number of large topics, or suggest another which he would like to
do. Topics suggested by our children were costume, ships, aircraft

and the cinema. Their suggestions involved the teacher in a good deal of preparatory work, but this was amply repaid by the enthusiasm and hard work the children put into them. Two of the girls, for example, working together on costume, became so engrossed that, after spending a year on the topic, they had only got as far as the late mediaeval period. The work, both written and artistic, was of a high order. The following was the card on which their work was based.

Costume
Read this card through carefully before you begin. These books will be useful to you:
Costume, P. Cunnington, Black.
The Ladybird Costume Book.
The Junior Heritage Book of Costume, James Laver, Batsford.
The Picture Reference Book of Costume, Kathleen Dance, Brockhampton.
Historical Costumes of England 1066–1956, Nancy Bradfield, Harrap.
Clothing and Costume, Dina P. Dobson, Longmans.
Costume, Brockhampton.
Costume through the Ages, James Laver. This book has many illustrations.
Historical Costuming, Truman, Pitmans.
English Costume, Doreen Yarwood, Batsford.
The library will have some very useful books on the subject. Look up 'Costume' in an encyclopaedia and make a note of any useful information. Find out if there are any other useful articles; read them, and make a note of the page numbers of information or pictures which you may need. Read *Costume* by P. Cunnington and the *Ladybird Costume Book*. You will now have a good general idea of what you are going to do. *Do not begin to write until you have planned what you intend to do and which pictures you are going to copy.* Write your account of costume, using the following chapters:
  1 Ancient Times (if you can find enough information)
  2 The Early Middle Ages (9th to 13th Centuries)
  3 The Later Middle Ages (14th and 15th Centuries)
  4 Tudor Times (16th Century)
  5 Stuart Times (17th Century)

6 Georgian Times (18th Century)
7 The Victorians (19th Century)
8 Modern Times (20th Century)

You will use many coloured pictures of costumes to illustrate your chapters. Design a coloured cover for your book. Put a neat contents page in the front, showing the page numbers of each chapter (you will have to number the pages of your book). Costume may be divided into four classes:

1 Clothes for leisure
2 Clothes for working
3 Clothes for fighting (armour or uniforms)
4 Clothes for sport (e.g. for football, athletics, hunting).

You should concentrate on the first two because armour and uniform are separate, very big, subjects and clothes for sport are, in general, a recent innovation.

Be sure that in each of your chapters you describe the dress of both rich and poor. If you can find any information about children's clothes, include this in the correct chapter. Do not merely copy from the text books. Make sure you understand what you are writing about; if you have any problems *ASK*.

The first cards were given to our children when they were eight years old but this kind of work could be begun with younger children who can read well. At the other end of the range, children of ten or eleven are not too old to make a start with simple cards, if such work is unfamiliar to them. They will of course work much more quickly and find satisfaction in giving fuller answers than those expected from younger children. However, it cannot be stressed too strongly that the first essential is to make the child familiar with the simple techniques of finding information before more ambitious work is attempted.

When the children had completed the basic forty cards, which took them between two and three years, they were given a free choice of subject. Any topic suggested had first to be examined to find out what suitable material might be available and the advice of the children's librarian at the public library was often sought. Some topics, such as 'Roman Britain' or 'Ships' had an almost embarrassing range of books to choose from but others proved unworkable because of the lack of books suitable for the children's use. It is important for a teacher to satisfy herself about the availability of suitable books before accepting a child's suggestion for a topic in order to save the child from discouraging frustration later. The cinema, for example, chosen by one of our boys proved difficult because of the shortage of simple texts on its history. At the other end of the scale, ships provided an embarrassment of riches and there were so many suitable books that the topic had to be divided into two: sailing ships and steam ships. Other topics chosen by the children were costume, space exploration, aircraft, castles, armour and Roman Britain. The last of these was suggested by the teacher to a boy who had already shown a special interest in history. He became so absorbed in it that he transformed what had been thought of as a topic for a term into a study lasting a year and a half, during the course of which he became an expert on the Roman legions in Britain and their movements. He turned to the Pelican edition of Caesar's *Commentaries* for information about the first Roman landing because, he said, it provided him with the fullest account and he later became interested in the lives of the Roman Emperors, adding a chronological list of them as a sort of appendix to his book. Other topics such as coal, oil, trains and motor cars were suggested to children who showed no strong preferences and were pursued with interest.

In all this work it is important that children should be quite clear that they are expected to report the information they gather in their own words and to understand what they write. Copying out passages from the books they read will not suffice and the teacher should satisfy herself on these points by questioning. At the same time, if a child finds it impossible to express an idea in his own words as clearly as it is given in the book, he should learn that he can quote from it, provided that he uses inverted commas and states his source. We did not expect our children to compile formal bibliographies, but they learned to make lists of the books they had consulted at the end of their work. One girl took this a stage further and compiled a simple index as well.

It is obvious that the topics selected for enquiry will reflect the teacher's own interests, but this does not matter so long as the children are interested in them and find their pursuit worthwhile. Whatever the topic, it is essential that the teacher should familiarize herself with the information available and assess its suitability for the children. This is bound to involve much work, but the children need guidance about the form their enquiries might take and about promising sources of information. A vague instruction to find out all he can about a given topic may well prove too daunting even for a clever child of this age and it runs the risk of causing unnecessary and undesirable frustration if he has no idea how to begin his enquiry, or is confronted at the outset by too difficult or unsuitable material. Although it is difficult for a busy class teacher to devote much time during the day to a clever child working on an extended topic of the kind described, it is essential that the child should be able to discuss his problems and questions with an interested adult. Clever children, if they are to be extended intellectually, need time to talk. They are full of questions which need answering: 'Does this collar turn up or down?'; 'How did this ship tack?'; 'Would a clothyard shaft penetrate plate armour?'; 'How were these tassels attached?'. As they get older they need to be shown that it is necessary to weigh evidence, to assess the reliability of different writers' accounts. All this needs individual attention and the teacher must find time, outside the timetable if necessary, to discuss the child's work with him if he is to derive the fullest benefit from the challenge it presents. As the children reach the age of ten or eleven they can pay useful visits to the reference section of a public library and they will soon become accustomed to using its facilities efficiently to gather information on topics which interest them.

Science

The preceding section of this chapter has been concerned with the efficient use of books for gathering information on topics in which the children are interested and with using and communicating the information. Careful observation and enquiry are developed in an experimental setting through science, to which we now turn.

As a background to what follows it is necessary to explain the limitations on the work with the children in our group on which this section is based. For the first two years the children occupied a classroom in which there was a sink with running water, but at the end of that time they moved to a classroom without that provision. Throughout the four years, they had the use of a small attic room as a workshop accommodating up to about six children at any one time. In addition, when it was not occupied by other classes, the children could use a room, known rather grandly in the school as the science room, which was equipped with several bunsen burners, tripods, retort stands, lengths of rubber tubing and miscellaneous glass tubing. Thus, the work described in this section took place without special science equipment or laboratory facilities, a situation not uncommon in primary schools. A further difficulty arose from our decision to put the teaching of science in the hands of a specialist who, owing to his other commitments, could usually visit the group for only one afternoon each week. Science, therefore, became a once a week activity with very little carry-over into the rest of the programme. A gap of one week between one part of a scientific investigation and another can destroy the interest of even highly motivated clever children. A minority of the group would quite willingly take up work left a week earlier but, on the whole, the effect was to place serious constraints upon the nature of the activities.

The weekly visit had the advantage of allowing time for careful preparation but the result of this, at first, was that the work was too closely directed by the teacher. In the last two years an attempt was made to achieve a balance between activities proposed and planned by the teacher and those arising from the children's own ideas. A science diary which was kept shows that the latter were increasingly used as a basis for individual or small group activity. The figures are given in Table 1. The lower figures for the autumn and summer terms in both years are partly accounted for by the fact that these were the times of year most suitable for outdoor work with a programme planned by the teacher. The diary shows clearly that during this period nine of the group of fifteen children were responsible for the ideas suggested and that about 40 per cent of them came from one boy (A). It is also interesting to compare the rather crude data in Table 1 with the scores of the children on interest inventories. The boys with the highest scores on the science items of the inventories were, on the whole, those who made the greatest number of suggestions for science activities. The pattern for the girls, however, was not as clear.

The increase in the number of activities based on the children's ideas was probably the result of a number of factors. Perhaps the most important was the growing realization on the part of the children that all ideas, no matter whether they were mundane or over-ambitious, would be welcomed and given serious consideration. This understanding between pupils and teacher is essential,

Table 1 Number of ideas suggested by children used as basis for science activities in the third and fourth years

Term	Third year children		Fourth year children	
Autumn	A 2	5	A 3	7
	B 1		C 2	
	C 1		J 1	
	D 1		K*1	
Spring	A 4	7	A 5	10
	D 1		F 2	
	E* 1		K 1	
	F 1		E 1	
			B 1	
Summer	A 1	4	A 2	6
	F 1		J 2	
	G 1		C 1	
	B 1		F 1	
Total no. of suggestions		16		23

* E and K are girls.

particularly if imaginative thinking is to be encouraged. Another factor was the widening of the children's concept of what was entailed in 'doing science'. In addition, as they got used to the idea of there being a weekly science afternoon, the children became more willing to save their scientific questions, whenever they arose, for that afternoon.

An important limitation of the science work with our children was of a more general nature. Very early, after several frustrating sessions, it was found that activities involving the whole group were unsatisfactory. All the children were not necessarily interested in doing science at the same time; discussion was difficult in the larger group; there was a wide range of individual differences in interest and understanding which added to the frustration. A pattern evolved therefore, of individual or small group work, four children being the maximum number involved on most occasions. A rota was, therefore, drawn up and the children made sure that it was adhered to. The composition of the small groups was arrived at in consultation with the class teacher and was based on our assessment of social and intellectual compatibility.

The chief advantage of such a system was that the teaching could be intensive and fitted to individual needs. The chief disadvantage was that the spasmodic nature of the contact did not help attempts to develop continuity and sequence. In the early days this manner of working was probably responsible for a lack of spontaneity in the responses of some of the children.

Aims and objectives

It would be pretentious to describe the work done in science with the gifted children as a curriculum development exercise. It would be more realistic to view the work as that of an individual teacher interested in exploring the possibilities of different approaches to science with a group of able children. At its lowest level, several hunches were assessed by the kind of intuitive professionalism employed daily by practising teachers. At its highest level, tentative hypotheses were tested by means of more sophisticated evaluation instruments devised by Mrs Wynne Harlen for use in the *Schools Council Science (5–13) Project*.

In spite of the small scale nature of the work, it was thought to be a salutary exercise to consider aims and objectives; an activity about which much has been written but very little communicated. Schwab (1969) sums up this situation when he describes writing on the curriculum as moribund and appeals for a 'practical language' with which to communicate. Taylor's (1970) survey of how teachers plan their courses reinforces this. He found that teachers could not discuss curriculum planning with any confidence and had little 'shared technical expertise' with which to facilitate communication. With this problem of communication, it is obviously necessary in considering aims and objectives to define what one is talking about. Aims are the long-term general intentions underlying an educational programme, while objectives are the more immediate goals or stages towards the realization of the long-term aims.

A good example of the use of aims and objectives in planning is to be found in the Schools Council publication *With Objectives in Mind* (1969). However, if too precisely defined in behavioural terms, objectives can, it has been claimed, become so restricting that they take the pleasure out of teaching. To avoid this, although we appreciated the value of carefully defined objectives in judging the balance, direction and effectiveness of teaching, we adopted a looser, more intuitive approach to science topics, based on a consideration of the principles and processes of scientific thinking.

The term 'science' is used for a wide range of activities. It is, for example, applied to the naive discoveries of a seven-year-old playing with magnets, to the activities of a sixteen-year-old repeating a well-worn experiment to show the properties of a gas, and to the original research of a professional scientist. Its use to describe all levels of sophistication can act as a barrier to communication for both teachers and children. Teachers of young children with little or no special background in science are often put off by the use of the word and may fail to recognize scientific elements in work they are already doing. Such teachers will probably feel considerable, and largely unwarranted anxiety when confronted with the prospect of providing science experiences for children known to be clever.

It is not only teachers for whom the word science can create difficulties. Children's conceptions of science are often over influenced by comics and television and there are many times when, like the teachers, they fail to realize that what they are doing has scientific aspects. During their early weeks with us, our children, then aged seven, were asked individually what they would like to do on the science afternoons. The following replies to the teacher's question are typical:

'What is science?'
'It's doing experiments and things—with chemistry and test-tubes. They work in laboratories.'
'It's about space and rockets. You do experiments—make stink bombs.'
'You find out about other planets—whether there's life. We could make a rocket.'

This conception of science either as a limited form of chemistry or romanticized space-exploration is far removed from many of the activities presented to children as sicence in an ordinary primary school setting. The challenge to the teacher of clever children is to present, in an appealing way, many of the more mundane activities which can form the basis of the children's growing scientific understanding.

In looking for a definition of science which has meaning for the
D

teaching of young children it is necessary to consider two elements in scientific activity:

1 A substantive element: a body of knowledge, information and principles that help us to understand the physical, biological and technological world around us.

2 A methodological element: a process or method of enquiry by which new information and principles are uncovered and old ideas discarded.

It is, of course, true that science as a method of enquiry cannot be taught without attention to content; method and substance are separable only for the purpose of discussion. It is, however, possible in teaching to emphasize the one or the other in any particular programme. The approach described here puts more emphasis on the methodological than on the substantive element in teaching science. It was concerned with man's natural and technological environment and the concepts, attitudes and skills useful in understanding and controlling it.

The children were encouraged to approach problems scientifically. This we assumed to entail the development of a set of attitudes and skills, many of which are not restricted solely to science teaching. The following summary indicates how they were covered in the programme.

1 The children were always encouraged to ask questions seeking information, interpretation and clarification. This was a 'natural' activity for most of the group. Questions, simple or sophisticated, were valued by the teacher. The questioning of the validity of evidence from whatever source, for example, teacher or reference book, was also encouraged.

2 Scientific activity often begins with simple observation. The children were encouraged to collect data systematically and to order and classify their observations.

3 Skills in interpreting data were encouraged. The children were often put in situations which required the interpretation of facts and ideas to arrive at a meaningful conclusion. They were also encouraged to accept the possibility of several valid interpretations from the same data. This attitude was consistently shown by only one child below the age of eight, but it was becoming a characteristic of a significant number of the group by the age of ten. A reasoned evaluation of different interpretations of scientific situations as

opposed to an emotional, often egocentric, one was still difficult for most of the children at the age of eleven.

4 After questions had been formulated, the children were often encouraged to devise experiments or investigations to answer them and examples of this kind of activity are described below. The opportunity to devise experiments for the purpose of solving problems is particularly important for clever children. After the initial formulation of questions the children were encouraged to

1 identify important variables;
2 devise some form of quantification or measurement for use in their investigation;
3 appreciate the need to control variables (even with clever children there is some evidence that this ability develops much later than eleven);
4 discover effective variables by investigation;
5 come some way towards the formulation and testing of hypotheses (not common even with clever children below the age of eleven).

5 The children were encouraged to communicate to others the results of their scientific investigations. Perhaps because science became a once a week activity, this aspect of the work was neglected. There was ready oral communication by most of the group but it became increasingly difficult to find time to work on different, more elaborate, forms of communication. It is, however, important to make time available for practising the writing of precise and accurate accounts of experiments as this is a valuable exercise in the use of language.

It will be seen that the encouragement of the skills and attitudes summarized above is part of the development of critical and analytical thinking which is not confined to scientific problems. In addition, we attempted to foster concern for contemporary environmental issues such as pollution and conservation, taking the point made by Schoenfeld (1970, p. 10) that 'it is unthinking people who pollute the environment, and it is thinking people who can bring about environmental conservation, redevelopment and maintenance'. Tackling such issues with children, a process which it is fashionable to call 'environmental education', can lead to the beginnings of understanding of ecosystems and the interdependence of man, animals and plant life.

Content

We have been chiefly concerned so far with introducing children to what is commonly called scientific method, but this cannot be done in a vacuum; some consideration needs to be given to content. For this purpose we made a list of a minimum number of important scientific ideas we thought should be introduced to our children and used the list, which follows, as a basis for the science programme.

1 The earth as an environment:
   Conditions which enable life to survive; the earth as a source of materials; the limited supply of materials; water on the earth; rocks; minerals; mountains; the air; weather and climate; weather forecasting; natural disasters.
2 The earth in the solar system:
   The planets; the moon; the stars; the universe.
3 Forms of life supported by the environment:
   Plants; animals; man as a social animal; simple methods of classification; life cycles; simple human biology; the senses.
4 The earth's resources:
   Conservation; pollution; interdependence of life; food chains.
5 Traditional content on energy and matter:
   Heat; electricity; magnetism; machines; friction; light; sound; an introduction to scientists' views about what things are made of.

There are many dangers in producing such a list and it should not be regarded as either exclusive or inclusive nor should it be taken as suggesting that there is one syllabus suitable for all clever children of this age group. Additions to and subtractions from it should be made according to a teacher's personal preferences and professional judgments. The list is descriptive, not prescriptive. It is included here to show how we approached the building of a science syllabus for our children. Teachers familiar with such lists in books on the teaching of elementary science will realize that there is nothing unusual about it. There is, indeed, no need to seek for unusual material in teaching science to clever children of seven to eleven, although both content and method need careful consideration.

Children's work

For science, as for much of the children's other work, we found it desirable to construct assignment cards setting tasks, problems and projects on the topics listed. The use of such cards with children of these ages is, of course, common; some teachers using published material, some adapting it to their own purposes, others preferring to make their own cards. The advantage of using cards is that the teacher can order the science experiences of her children and knows beforehand the apparatus likely to be needed while, at the same time, allowing for individual differences in pace and interest. On the other hand it can be objected that science work should arise from the children's questions rather than the teacher's and that the programme, at this stage, should be based on their questions and interests in science at the time. To do this, not only demands a knowledgeable teacher working in a highly flexible system, but it also assumes that the children will pose questions which it is practicable and profitable for them to investigate. These assumptions did not seem warranted for our children and we, therefore, attempted to achieve a balance between teacher direction and children's interests. The children were persistent questioners on matters scientific and many issues in which they became deeply involved arose from a question in a book, a television programme, or an assignment card.

The science assignment cards used were either specially written or adapted from published materials. It is difficult to generalize about the children's reactions to them but our impression was that they were not popular. Most of the group would work through the cards willingly but without much enthusiasm. A small section of the group, in particular the divergent thinkers, were openly bored by any systematic use of science cards, although different versions of cards on the same theme were experimented with in attempts to allow for maximum flexibility of response. It is also interesting to note that, from the outset, we found the same reluctance on the part of our children to record their experiments as was found by Bridges and his colleagues with the children at Brentwood. It is possible that this reluctance sprang from the fact that science was only a weekly activity for both sets of children.

Throughout the four years of our work it proved much more difficult to motivate the girls than the boys in science. A diary of the weekly science sessions contains many examples of scientific naivety on the part of the girls. At the age of seven to eight most of the boys could, working from assignment cards, make quite complex electrical circuits and experiment with them while, at the same age, two of the girls were fascinated and astounded when, having constructed a simple circuit, they caused a bulb to light. Another girl attempted to make a circuit with string and then, realizing she had to use wire, failed to make a circuit because she did not realize that plastic cable had to be stripped to bare the wire.

To sum up, our experience of using science assignment cards with the group suggests that, while they can provide a useful framework for science activity, they should not be the only stimulus used. For our children, the best cards were those providing as many open-ended situations as possible. The format of the cards should be varied and they should be clearly related to practical science activities. The danger is that some cards may be little more than the equivalent of standard textbooks presented a page at a time. We made this mistake with some of our early cards and the children were bored by them. Finally, there are some gifted children who, despite an obvious interest in science, fail to react to science assignment cards no matter what form they take. Our group contained a boy of this kind. To him, science was a lively, active, tactile and practical activity. The ability of this boy to express his scientific ideas through models, gadgets and 'Heath-Robinson' devices improved during his four years in the class, but the gap between his thinking and his 'technology' always remained a source of frustration to him. To tie such a child to science assignment cards is an insult. He, almost invariably, had more scientific ideas than the people around him, including the adults.

Another possible resource at the disposal of a teacher faced with the problem of providing for the exceptional abilities of one or two clever children in a class of thirty or forty is the use of programmed material either in the form of a programmed text or for use with a simple teaching machine. In recent years, changes in thinking about programmed learning have resulted in a movement away from the rather arid, highly behaviouristic type of material, which a clever child finds frustrating, to a less rigid approach based upon the learning of concepts and processes. A machine is not essential for the presentation of a programme but, particularly with young children, there can be advantages in using one. Its novelty gives it a very strong initial appeal for many children although this effect weakens with familiarity of use. Machines are also more cheat proof than texts and most of them provide a complete record of correct and incorrect responses on completion of the programme.

To gain some idea of the advantages and limitations of programmed learning in science with clever children we provided a simple machine, the 'Tutorpak', for our children's use when they were eight to nine years old. Some of the science programmes had accompanying materials for related practical activities but there was not enough of this material and our children did not find it sufficiently attractive. It is, of course, well known that programmes vary enormously and much careful study of the details of validation and of the populations with which a programme has been developed is necessary before buying it.

Our children found the machine easy to use and easy to load. Although loading was supposed to be done by the teacher lest the children should see the answers to the next series of questions, we found this to be unimportant because the children's attention was so much concentrated on loading that they took little notice of the answers and the results were, therefore, very little affected.

The first science programme used was an introduction to the centre of gravity which is part of a series including a programme on falling bodies. 'Centre of Gravity I' uses only two terms, 'force' and 'mass', which depend on previous programmes and as these come in adjoining recapitulation frames, the programme can be used independently. It is devised for children aged twelve to thirteen, that is, four years older than ours at the time. The following extract from the science teacher's diary describes the use of the programme by two of our boys, A and B.

A had not used the Tutorpak before but was able to load it easily and soon learned where he was to write. After initial confusion about reference to the accompanying text which had a diagrammatic representation of a brick in three positions and a cone, he worked quickly. To aid scoring and to reinforce correct answers, he was instructed to put 1 on his paper for a correct response and 0 for an error. Although he generally remembered to do this, the number of times he omitted to do so is probably an indication that this practice was not really necessary for him. He knew how well or how badly he was doing without a written tally. He completed the programme in fifty-one minutes with four errors. His errors were all similar, involving the concept of area of support and its relationship to centre of gravity. He was confused about the effect of centre of gravity over, inside, or outside the area of support but the final eight frames secured his understanding and the immediate recall test showed a 90 per cent level of recall. He appeared to be interested in the programme and in trying to understand the concepts involved. He enjoyed using the machine and his only criticism was 'you can not write properly with it'. By this he meant that the space in which each answer was to be written was small and not well supported, thus making it difficult to write normally. For A, who was not the tidiest of recorders, this was an interesting comment.

Contrast this with the description of B using the same programme.

B loaded the machine easily. He was keen, tense, bubbly, verbalizing all the time. He soon appreciated the need to look at the text sheet. He was interested in marking 1 or 0 after his responses and saw the programme as a challenge to his ego. 'How many 0s did A get?' he asked. He worked through the programme much more slowly than A, probably because of his self-generated competitive anxiety. He seemed to be less interested in the scientific concepts than in the sounds of the words he was using. When presented with a problem of which he was unsure, he interchanged 'gravity', 'force' and 'mass' until they sounded right. He made five errors but his immediate recall score was 55 per cent which indicated his lack of understanding of the science involved and strengthened the impression that he was merely learning a form of words. He completed the programme in 68 minutes.

In this and subsequent sessions both boys were fully involved with the programmed material but the above descriptions show the danger of taking the depth of involvement as the sole indicator of its effectiveness. It is probably true to say that A was thinking and learning science whereas the programme did little to develop the scientific understanding of B. Examples from the use of a wide range of science programmes with other children in the group could be quoted to support the same point. Programmes, even with gifted children, can be used to keep children occupied but with little evidence of effective learning taking place. It would appear, therefore, that the results of post-programme tests should not be taken as the sole means of assessing their value. Time must be found for talking to the children if a much wider assessment is to be made of the kind of learning that has taken place.

Programmed material and teaching machines can, however, be useful aids in teaching clever children, if the programmes are chosen carefully and used with discrimination. An example of their effectiveness was shown when one of the boys became interested in chemical symbols and formulae. He worked quickly and effectively through a programmed text incorporating the use of a Stillitron machine. The text used a multiple-choice technique. When the correct response was marked with a sensitive 'pencil', a circuit was completed and a green light shone, thus giving immediate reinforcement. The boy enjoyed doing this and very quickly acquired the skill required to use chemical formulae. Programmes used in this way can provide individual teaching and testing situations and, thus, relieve the pressures upon a teacher's time and energy.

Science and the environment

The environment is a natural extension of the classroom and is full of resources for science teaching. Our children were taken out of school regularly throughout the four years as part of a normal school programme aimed at familiarizing them with the local environment and as part of a policy to provide them with enrichment experiences. For our children, at school in a seaside town, the obvious starting points for science outside the classroom were the street, local parks, the beach, a patch of waste ground and a nearby railway line. Most of the activities which developed from these starting points are common-place in primary schools but some examples may be of interest.

The street

This was in an early twentieth-century inner suburb.

Activities—Studying the use of a variety of building materials and building techniques. One boy became fascinated by trying to discover the strengths of different brick bonds.
Contrasting gardens in the sun and gardens in the shade. One group calculated that a particular garden only had four hours of sunshine during the time of year when a survey was conducted; another group studied plants that grow in the sun and plants that grow in the shade; another studied mosses and lichens found growing on walls.

Local parks

There were two examples of late Victorian parks within a short distance of the school.

Activities—The study of trees including tree spreads; the life-cycle of trees; the bird life in the park (mainly mallards and geese).

Although it is probably true that many teachers under-estimate the capabilities of gifted children, it is sometimes possible to over-estimate them. Most of the work planned for the visits to the parks in the early days proved to be too ambitious. In this natural science environment, many of the children displayed an ignorance of the names of common wild flowers and trees. Some of them reacted with incredibility and amazement when they were told that the hundreds of 'little plants' growing under and around a sycamore were seeds from the parent tree. 'Do all trees grow from seeds?' asked one girl. Perhaps such a situation simply reflects the movement away from nature study to science in the curriculum of young children, but examples like these emphasize the fact that children can be both clever and ignorant.

The beach

The beach was large and sandy.

Activities—There is little point in listing, in any detail, the scientific activities which arose naturally from a visit to the beach. Typical ones included studying tide levels; collecting shells and other 'debris' from the tide line; examining sea water. A piece of waste land near the school proved useful when introducing sampling techniques such as quadrats and transects. A nearby railway signal box was a favourite place for a visit and provided a fund of scientific stimuli.

One or two of the girls were difficult to motivate in science but it was interesting to observe that sex differences in terms of interest and achievement were less obvious when the children were engaged in this type of environmental science than they were in other science activities.

It is easy to come to think of curriculum enrichment in science solely in terms of out-of-school activities but serious attention should also be given to enrichment inside the classroom. Where circumstances allow, this may take the form of a generous provision of equipment, but a careful choice must be made, as sophisticated scientific apparatus may prove undesirable. Children aged seven to eleven, even clever ones, are unlikely to be ready for it and it is possible that premature acquaintance with such apparatus will take away some of the thrill and interest when it is encountered later. The provision of a wide range of good quality reference books is another form of classroom enrichment. Well written, well illustrated science books by acknowledged experts can stimulate thinking and enhance understanding. Our children had access to a wide range of reference books and encyclopaedias which brought to them, for example, the world of astronomy, rockets, space travel, radio telescopes, radar and laser beams. A few of the boys were regular viewers of a television programme entitled 'Tomorrow's World' and were often quick to point out how scientific ideas, even in a recently published book, can become outmoded.

Much stress, in our science teaching, was laid on developing problem-solving strategies. Small groups of children would be encouraged to explore a particular situation by thinking aloud, making predictions and then testing them. On one occasion, for example, the children were provided with four polystyrene balls of different sizes and a ramp set at a given gradient. Each child was asked to predict which ball would be quickest down the ramp and to give the reasons for his view. The children then tested their predictions experimentally and, if they were wrong, as they often were, they were faced with the problem of finding why they were mistaken. They repeated the experiment with ball-bearings of different sizes and also investigated the effect of change of gradient.

On another occasion a small group set out to test the reactions of the rest of the class by using a simple measuring device. After discussion they found that different testers got different results. Further questioning and discussion resulted in the group investigating how testing in private and before an audience affected reactions. On both these occasions the science activity could be described as humdrum but the discussion arising was enriching. Much is written about learning science by doing but, in our experience, particularly in the last year of our work when most of the children were almost eleven, a significant number of the boys enjoyed thinking about science without necessarily doing anything.

Evaluation

Although it was not possible for us to attempt a sophisticated evaluation of our science teaching, an opportunity was taken to use some of the evaluation instruments devised by Mrs Wynne Harlen for the Schools Council science (5 to 13) project. These were: a general test; a test of concepts related to metals; a test of concepts related to time.

The unusual format of these tests, which appealed to the children, needs to be described. In each test the children were presented with a filmed sequence of some scientific activity about which they were asked questions. The films were presented using an 8 mm loop projector which allowed any frame to be held in still form. A commentary and detailed instructions for administration were provided with each test. The children, tested in groups, were required to write their responses, usually of the multiple choice variety, in an accompanying booklet. All three tests were given to the children at the age of ten. It was intended to repeat them at the end of their fourth year (age eleven), but the results obtained on first application of the metals and time tests were so high that there was little headroom for improvement. Consequently, only the general test was repeated.

The results of the applications of the general test are given in Table 2. The test has four sections, each section being related to a set of objectives. The scores of the gifted children were contrasted with those of the national sample for both test and re-test and, as would be expected, were found to be significantly superior. The group scored so highly on three of the four sections that they had little headroom for improvement and the mean percentage score in section 4 for the re-test showed a slight deterioration. In section 3, the gifted children, in common with the national sample, registered their lowest scores. Throughout our science teaching considerable emphasis had been placed upon the need to identify and control the variables operating in any situation but, despite this, the children's scores suggest that there was considerable room for improvement. Following the test, direct attempts to develop 'thinking strategies' in relation to scientific problems were intensified and this may account for the improvement shown in this section in the re-test. On the other hand, the improvement may have occurred regardless of the emphasis in the teaching and may be attributable to the move from 'describer' to 'explainer' thinking (Peel, 1967) involved in the development of formal operations.

Table 2 Scores of gifted children compared with those of a national sample (scores expressed as percentages)

Section	Objectives	Max. mark	National sample test	National sample re-test	Gifted children test	Gifted children re-test
1	Ability to predict the effect of certain changes through observation of similar changes Awareness that more than one variable may be involved in a particular change	4	54·9	64·5	82·1	92·4
2	Ability to tabulate information and use tables. Ability to use representational symbols for recording information on charts	6	71·6	82·5	91·6	95·8
3	Appreciation of the need to control variables and use controls in investigations Ability to investigate variables and to discover effective ones	5	33·6	41·1	57·1	67·3
4	Ability to use non-representational symbols in plans, charts etc. Ability to use histograms and other simple graphical forms for communicating data	6	57·6	75·1	95·2	93·6

During the four years other less sophisticated attempts at evaluation were attempted. For example, at the end of the first year, when most of the children were eight years old, several questions of a scientific nature were asked of the children in individual interview situations. The same questions were repeated three years later. In most cases the responses at eleven showed substantial increases in understanding. As an illustration, in response to the questions, 'What is sound?', 'How is it caused?', at eight only five of the eight-year-old children were able to say that sound was caused by something vibrating, whereas twelve of the group gave acceptable answers at the age of eleven. On the other hand, in response to the question 'What is a magnet?' there was little evidence of improvement in individual responses between ages eight and eleven.

A (*girl*)

At age eight: 'A magnet is like a horseshoe. It is iron. It draws other iron things to it.'
At age eleven: 'A magnet is a metal bar. It attracts another steel or metal object towards it.'

B (*boy*)

At age eight: 'A magnet is a metal bar which attracts other metal. I think it is painted with some special stuff to make it work.'
At age eleven: 'A magnet is an instrument which attracts metal. It is covered with something, probably a chemical, which attracts metal.'

C (*boy*)

At age eight: 'A magnet is a piece of metal which other metals stick to, but not brass, copper and aluminium. It's got electric in it or it's covered with something to make it work.'
At age eleven: 'A magnet is a piece of metal which, when applied to other metals, the other metals stick to it. A magnet works like this if it is first coated with a special substance which makes it magnetic. You can make another magnet by rubbing some of this substance on to the surface of another piece of metal.'

The myth about the chemical coating was widespread within the group.

Some of the children were unusually able to use the technical language of science but it was necessary to check that they understood the meaning of many of the words they used. A small group of boys who had become interested in radio constructed an effective crystal set after buying the necessary parts from a local shop. They then amplified the sound through the speaker of a tape-recorder and learned how to vary the wave length and how to select different stations. After this they became interested in transistors and simple electronics kits. As a result of these experiences, they began to use words such as 'fuse', 'valve', 'amplifier', 'diode', 'transistor' and 'resistor' in a way which impressed many people who saw them at work. Close questioning, however, revealed very limited understanding of many of the words they were using. When asked 'Why are you using a diode here?', the response was 'because it says so in the book' or 'because the man in the shop said I had to'. The boys were, undoubtedly, learning a great deal from their activity but the perceptive teacher would not be over-impressed by this and would hope to improve the quality of the work by getting them to examine the words they were using. Our children responded positively to challenging questioning and showed clearly that they not only enjoyed 'doing' science, but that they also enjoyed 'thinking' science.

Material on science teaching

The following are some of the publications on teaching elementary science in which teachers will find ideas capable of being adapted for use with clever children between the ages of seven and eleven. It is not, of course, suggested that the list is in any way exhaustive and experienced teachers will know many, or all, of the items, but teachers new to the problems we have been discussing may find it a useful starting point.

Armstrong, H. E. (1910), *The Teaching of Scientific Method and Other Papers on Education*, Macmillan, London.

Association for Science Education. (1967), *Science and Education. Science in the Introductory Phase: Three Teaching Schemes for the Introduction of Science in the Junior Forms of Secondary Schools*, Murray, London.

Association for Science Education. (1971), *Science and General Education*, Hatfield, Herts.

Association for Science Education. (1966), *Science for Primary Schools. 1. Children Learning through Science. 2. List of Books. 3. List of Teaching Aids*, Murray, London.

Association for Science Education. (1967), *Science Teaching Techniques*, *12*, Murray, London.

Association for Science Education. (1970), *Using Broadcasts*, Murray, London.

Blackwell, F. F. (1968), *Starting Points for Science—1*, Blackwell, Oxford.

Blough, G. O. and Schwartz, J. (1964), *Elementary School Science and How to Teach it*, Holt, Rinehart & Winston, New York.

Cheshire Education Committee. (1967), *Science in the Primary School*, University of London Press.

Gega, P. C. (1966), *Science in Elementary Education*, Wiley, New York.

Jacobson, W. J. and Tannenbaum, H. E. (1961), *Modern Elementary School Science: A Recommended Sequence*, Teachers' College, Columbia, New York.

James, A. (1960), *Science in the Junior School (the Teachers' Guide to the Natural Science Series)*, Schofield & Sons, Huddersfield.

Laybourn, K. and Bailey, C. H. (1971), *Teaching Science to the Ordinary Pupil*, University of London Press.

Lee, E. C. (1967), *New Developments in Science Teaching*, Wadsworth Publishing Co., Belmont, California.

Ministry of Education. (1961), *Science in Primary Schools*, HMSO.

Nature Conservancy. (1963), *Science out of Doors: A Report of the Study Group on Education and Field Biology*, Longmans, London.

Nuffield Junior Science Project, (1967), *Nuffield Junior Science: Teachers' Guide*, Collins, London.

Redman, S., Brereton, Anne, Boyers, P. (1969), *An Approach to Primary Science: A Book for Teachers of Juniors and Infants*, Macmillan, London.

Renner, J. W. and Ragan, W. B. (1968), *Teaching Science in the Elementary School*, Harper & Row, New York.

Romey, W. D. (1968), *Inquiry Techniques for Teaching Science*, Prentice-Hall, Englewood Cliffs, New Jersey.

Schools Council. (1970), *Changes in School Science Teaching*, Evans, London.

Selberg, Edith M., Neal, Louise A., Vessel, M. F. (1970), *Discovering Science in the Elementary School*, Addison-Wesley, Reading, Mass.

Tricker, R. A. R. (1967), *The Contribution of Science to Education,* Mills & Boon, London.

UNESCO. (1962), *Source Book for Science Teaching.*

Victor, E. (1965), *Science for the Elementary School,* Macmillan, New York.

Wilson, R. W. (1968), *Useful Addresses for Science Teachers,* Arnold, London.

E

Problem solving

4

Logical reasoning

It may seem strange to find a section, even a short one, headed 'logical reasoning' and separated from the discussion of such activities as science and mathematics. It is, of course, obvious, that the separation is made only for the purpose of discussion as opportunities for the development of clear and logical thinking occur in every lesson no matter what the topic may be. Nevertheless, there are some occasions and some activities which are regarded as particularly useful for this purpose and prominent among them are those labelled science and mathematics. The teacher can not, however, assume that the child who is clever at designing experiments and drawing conclusions from them or in solving problems in mathematics will bring the same quality of logical reasoning to bear on other everyday problems or will be immune to specious arguments. Nor does it seem safe to assume that this more general application of logical reasoning can safely be left to chance; that it will be exercised and developed as and when occasions arise. A teacher will make full use of such occasions whenever she is able to do so but, in our work with clever children, it seemed to us desirable to supplement this use by providing material which would require and stimulate careful reasoning, but which the children would not regard as either 'science' or 'mathematics'.

The starting point for logical reasoning lies in clear, accurate expression involving close attention to the meanings of words. Clever children soon learn to spot ambiguities and enjoy doing so and can be brought from seeing them in the statements of others to looking for them in their own. A well known and useful exercise to this end is for the teacher to draw a diagram of a rectangular room, indicating the positions of door, window, fireplace or radiator, a table and chairs in the centre of the room and, perhaps, a sideboard or bookcase, or both, against a wall. The child's task is to write a short description of the room and its contents as seen by a person standing in the doorway. He is warned that, when the teacher draws the diagram from his description, she will take advantage of any imprecision or ambiguity, with the result that the original diagram will only be re-drawn if the child's description is accurate and unambiguous. Children enjoy occasional exercises of this kind which focus their attention on the importance of choosing the right word for the right place. There are many variations on this exercise and it can easily be simplified or made more complicated. Giving directions how to do or make things is a common exercise emphasizing the importance of orderly sequence.

Other useful material, as every teacher knows, abounds in advertisements and bright children are soon able to appreciate the absurdity of the claims made in some of them. That something can be made whiter than white, for example, is quickly recognized for the absurdity that it is. Other claims are quickly recognized as spurious when the child brings his mathematical or scientific knowledge to bear on them. The findings of best buys, for example, among packages of varying size and weight presents a mathematical problem. Less obviously mathematical are problems such as this:

> The boys and girls in a class had been comparing their spending money and they found that the average was 25p a week. Susan, Jane, Tom, Jim and Peter were very indignant when they got home because they were getting less than the average. All their fathers, except Peter's, were sympathetic and readily agreed to raise the spending money to 25p. Peter's father, however, said he could not afford to raise his spending money to the average because, in the end, he might have to give him 40p a week, the amount received by John and George who got the most money in the class. Was Peter's father right or wrong? Why?

The following is another, and to some extent allied, problem which interested our children:

> 'More people in London than in any other city have won the £25,000 premium bond prize,' said Jim to Tom. 'We are going to live in London,' he went on, 'so we shall have a better chance of winning the prize than we should have if we stayed here in Sheffield.' Was Jim right? Why?

The children may not at first appreciate that the next problem is connected with their work on sets:

'Most boys wear jackets and most boys wear pullovers, therefore, most boys wear both.' Do you think that the conclusion in this statement is true? What are the reasons for your answer?

Problems related to scientific thinking and experiment are another kind which can be posed. This example is concerned with the selection of data:

Peter was helping his father in the garden when he dropped two nails, one eight centimetres long and the other four. The next morning he found the nails and the eight centimetre nail had become rusty but not the four centimetre one. What facts would you need to know before you could explain this?

The next sets a problem in designing an experiment:

'Buy Evarite pens; they last longer than other pens of the same price. They go on writing for miles and miles.' This is an advertisement for 'Evarite' ball-point pens. What would you do to prove whether or not this claim is correct?

Boys, particularly, are interested in what might be called strategic problems and the possibilities here are endless. The first of the series of cards we designed for our children to promote logical thinking was one of these. It shows a DR 1 (1917) triplane in flight, front and side views, and the problem is given as follows:

This is the DR 1 triplane which had three wings. It could climb very quickly; much quicker than the British fighters of that time. It was also very fast in level flight, but not so good in a dive; sometimes, in a steep dive the top wing broke off.
1 If you were a British airman attacked by a triplane, how would you try to escape?
2 If you were flying a triplane and a British airman got on your tail, how would you try to escape?

It will be seen that this problem requires the children to take careful note of several characteristics and to assess them from opposing points of view in the two questions. The drawings of the triplane attracted interest and this was maintained by the problems set which appealed to the children as being 'real'. There were a number of similar cards in the series. Cards with information on maps setting problems of attack and defence were also popular as were problems of where a tribe would be likely to settle in a mapped piece of country, what they would have to offer to trade and so on. Another example, on a card with a drawing of a shipwreck, posed this problem:

You are on a ship which strikes a rock near an island in the Pacific Ocean. The rest of the crew have sailed away in a large lifeboat, leaving you on your own. You have a small life raft which could carry two people. The island has fresh water, coconut trees and there are some goats living on it. You have just enough time to collect one load of supplies before the ship sinks. What items would be most useful to you?

Another popular card set a problem in shunting in order to make up a railway goods train with its wagons in a specified order. A drawing of the made up train with its wagons in the correct order was shown with a plan of the sidings below. The wagons needed for the train were in colour to distinguish them from the others in the sidings and they were numbered. The directions read:

At the top of the card is a train of wagons. The train must be made up of the wagons in the order shown. At present the wagons, coloured red, are parked with others in three sidings. The shunter must arrange the red wagons in the right order on the main line. Draw a plan of the railway sidings and describe the way the shunter could sort them into order, so that the locomotive, which is on the loop line, can pull them away.

Another kind of exercise, involving the assessment of character can be made up from short personal descriptions. The following is an example:

Choosing the right man
Below are the descriptions of three men, Anson, Barlow and Chapman, who are applying to be captain of a large airliner. Say which man you would choose for the job and why you consider the other two less suitable.
Anson: Height 6ft 3in, weight 182 lb; fair hair, blue eyes, very attractive; very good eyesight; a good games player; brave but

reckless at times; a very good pilot who flew Spitfires during the war; very cheerful.

Barlow: Height 5ft 11in, weight 175 lb; dark hair slightly balding, brown eyes; good eyesight; quiet and not easily excited; an experienced pilot who was a navigator during the war; a cautious man.

Chapman: Height 5ft 10in, weight 174 lb; black curly hair, grey eyes; wears contact lenses; a kind man who loves animals but sometimes impatient with people; experienced pilot of transport planes; makes quick decisions and likes to be in charge of things.

Problems of this kind call for decision on which characteristics are relevant and an assessment of their comparative importance in making the final choice. Another kind of problem in character assessment involves not only weighing evidence but distinguishing fact from impression, as in this example:

Tom
Mother: 'Tom is always a good boy.'
Father: 'He's a real lad, always up to mischief, but he would never do anything really wrong.'
Vicar: 'Tom is in the choir and comes to Sunday school regularly.'
Tom's former teacher: 'Tom is not trustworthy; he never tells the truth.'
Policeman: 'He gave a false name and address.'
Tom's friend: 'Tom's a fine fellow.'
Tom's employer: 'Tom and his friend stole some money.'
The next-door neighbour: 'He never had a chance, with friends as bad as those he had.'
Tom: 'I ain't done nothing wrong.'
Here you have nine pieces of evidence. Say how much you would believe each one and then sum up your impression of Tom.

There are many other kinds of exercise, such as those based on careless understanding, as, for example:

'You said, yesterday, it might snow to-day, but it hasn't done, so you were wrong,' said John to Kate. What was Kate's answer?

All these examples illustrate the kind of reasoning exercises our children found taxing and interesting from their second year, age eight, onwards. Although not easy to devise, a number of them have been given in the hope that they will help teachers to construct more for their pupils. Wherever illustrations are appropriate, as in the 'strategic' examples given, they should be added, as they provide an immediate appeal to the interest of the children doing the exercises. In our own cards, we made liberal use of coloured drawings wherever possible. As their appreciation of ambiguity and false reasoning develops, children can be encouraged to bring examples they come across in their reading or conversation for examination in class. Clever children often show an interest in the reasons for saying or doing things from an early age and, from this beginning, the practice of examining their own and other's statements can be fostered in school when they are quite young.

Mathematics

It would be a mistake to expect that because a child is highly intelligent, he will do well at mathematics. Two of our girls, for example, were not in any way mathematically inclined, one being completely and cheerfully uninterested in anything to do with numbers and the other so convinced that she could not do mathematics that it proved impossible to persuade her otherwise. A teacher should not, therefore, be upset if an exceptionally intelligent child in her class gives an average or even below average performance in mathematics.

At the other extreme two of our boys were outstanding. One of them was, from the first year, particularly interested in patterns. Given a random series of numbers, he would try to relate them to one another and, at one time, mystified his teacher by devising number patterns as answers to his sums. The other boy would do his best only when he believed that the problems he was attempting were more difficult than those attempted by any other child in the group.

Thus, individual assignments soon became essential, even with a group of children of IQ 130 and above, and a teacher must expect wide variation in rates of progress, resulting in marked disparities in performance by the age of eleven. The best children at this age may be able to solve problems considered suitable for the average sixteen-year-old, while others are no more able than the average child of eleven. Working at their own pace is bound to emphasize individual differences, but there can be no excuse for holding back the able in the interests of apparent equality.

We planned the work in four sections and each assignment contained a component from each section: formal work based on a published series of mathematics books for children of seven to eleven; practical work, also based on a published series of work books; a series of about one hundred cards devised by the teacher on topics in algebra and another series, by the teacher, of about sixty cards on practical geometry. In addition, in the second year, age eight to nine, every child did a programme on calculating machines covering addition and subtraction, multiplication and division of whole numbers and decimals, and continuous multiplication, using the transfer key. During the fourth year, the more advanced children did programmes on trigonometry and the use of the slide rule, and two boys found interest and enjoyment in working through a large part of the companion exercises to F. W. Land, *The Language of Mathematics*.

In the first year, the number line, balance bar, play money, 'Soma' blocks (Gardner, 1966) and 'Multiboard' proved interesting and useful. Dienes MAB apparatus was provided as a means of developing the idea of a number base, but for some reason it was not a success. The children were unwilling to use the wooden blocks in their calculation and, without them, forgot what number base they were using. It is possible that either the method or the timing of the introduction of this apparatus was at fault. The children were not in the least unwilling to use other apparatus, particularly if the pieces gave the impression of being solid and substantial. A chess set with large pieces which could be moved with a convincing sound proved much more popular than smaller sets. Chess is, of course, a good exercise in reasoning and forward planning and able children often find its challenge exciting. It was very popular with ours in the first year but was abandoned in the second. It re-appeared in the third and fourth years, but its popularity was then confined to the best mathematicians, one or two of whom could play a very good game.

The series of cards devised to introduce algebra began with sets and the children knew them by that name. The early cards aimed at familiarizing them with the language and symbols commonly used and it was soon possible to ask such questions as:

If x = {7, 8, 9, 10, 11} which of the following sets is a subset of
x: (a) {7, 9} (b) {9, 10, 11, 12} (c) {9, 7, 10, 8}
(d) {6 + 1, 8, 8 + 1}?
Are you a subset of your class?
Is your class a subset of classes in your school?
Are you a subset of your family?
Is your family a subset of your class?

The ideas of subsets, common elements, complementary sets, one
to one correspondence and the use of sets in the classification of
information and solving of problems were covered. Card number
fifteen in the series of about a hundred, is an example of the kind of
exercise the children found interesting and challenging at this early
stage.

Card number 15
Class 2E

Name	Age	Height	Hair colour	Eye colour	Type of home	Father's job
Tom Able	10	4ft 6in	brown	brown	house	plumber
Peter Baker	9½	4ft 7in	fair	blue	flat	chemist
John Charles	9¾	4ft 10in	red	green	house	grocer
William Dobson	10¼	4ft 9in	brown	green	caravan	house painter
Oscar Eason	9½	4ft 8in	fair	hazel	flat	bank manager
Peter Fox	10	4ft 11in	fair	blue	bungalow	teacher
Norman Howe	9¾	4ft 9in	brown	hazel	house	dustman
Joseph Jig	10	5ft 0in	fair	green	flat	labourer
Brian King	9¾	4ft 9in	red	blue	house	farmer
Ian Leese	10	4ft 2in	brown	brown	flat	policeman
Philip Makin	9¼	4ft 3in	fair	blue	house	farm worker
Paul Noaks	10	4ft 8in	brown	hazel	house	solicitor
Mary Dodd	9½	4ft 7in	brown	hazel	flat	gardener
Pauline Fox	10	4ft 11in	fair	blue	bungalow	teacher
Jean Hoskin	9½	5ft 1in	brown	green	house	mechanic
Pauline Jones	9½	5ft 2in	fair	blue	house	postman

Name the members of the following sets:

Set A {all the fair-haired boys in the class} =
Set B {all the girls who live in houses} =
Set C {all the twins} =
Set D {the children aged exactly 10 years} =
Set E {children less than 4ft 8in tall} =
Set F {boys with blue eyes and fair hair} =

If Set G is {all the girls}, what is Set G–Set B?
What is A ∪ B?
What is D–F?
What is A–F?
What do the fathers of fair-haired flat-dwelling children do for a living?
If set J = {children living in bungalows} and Set K = {children living in caravans} what is J ∪ K?
What is D ∩ E?
If X = {the whole class} and Y = {all children who live in a house}, X − Y = ?

Next followed work on open sentences, replacement sets and inequalities. Succeeding cards then dealt with the powers of numbers, the collection of terms for addition and multiplication and simple equations. A card half-way through the series contained a number of exercises in finding hidden numbers, for example: $x + 7 = 12$;

$y - 13 = 12$; $3x = 12$; $\dfrac{c}{3} = 12$; $3z + 4 = 19$; $q^2 + 12 = 28$;

$b + p = 13$; $12c + 8c - 3c = 68$; $3\left(\dfrac{8+4}{6}\right) + 5 = q$; $z^3 = 216$;

$20 > y > 17$; $6m + 5 = -13$; $z^2 = \dfrac{4(\frac{12}{3}) + 3(14 - 9) + 9}{10}$

The card warned the children that an answer might show that more than one hidden number was denoted by the letter.

Directed numbers were difficult even for children of this ability and particularly, of course, for the less mathematically inclined. These were easily baffled by such questions as: 'If you owe me £5 and £2 and I take away your debt of £2, you are better off. Is this true? What do you now owe?' Or, again: 'If I take away twice your debt, you are twice as well off. Is this true? If your debt was £5, what is your position now?' As many as ten cards in the series had to be devoted to developing an understanding of the meaning of negative numbers.

The next topic, which was also the subject of a long series of cards, was multiplication systems, covering some early methods, the binary system, Napier's rods and logarithms. Some of the boys in particular found the binary system had attractions similar to those of writing in a secret code and they were quick to notice any mistake in the number or position of 1 and 0 in the binary equivalent of a large decimal system number. They got a great deal of pleasure out of finding occasional mistakes of this kind in the teacher's answers. Napier's rods led to logarithms and it was interesting to find that one boy, who, although mathematically competent, often seemed to lack interest, worked through a programme on logarithms with a Stillitron with considerable enthusiasm and very few mistakes. Moreover, he proved that he was able to use logarithms in various calculations afterwards.

Other cards in the series continued the work on equations to include problems requiring familiarity with the use of simultaneous equations. Manual calculating machines were provided for the children in the second year (age eight to nine), and an instructional series of cards was written, the first of which contained a diagram showing clearly the various levers and registers and simple instructions on their use followed by a number of additions to be done for practice. Visual explanation of this kind is necessary if children are working individually as it will be found that many able children can relate the diagram and instructions to the machine without help, thus leaving the teacher free to attend to those who have difficulties. Our children found working with these machines very interesting and soon became proficient in their use. The programme devised took them through addition, subtraction, multiplication and division of whole numbers and decimals and continuous multiplication, using the transfer key. Once they were proficient, the children were allowed to use the machines for long routine calculations whenever they wished. They enjoyed competitive speed trials and staged contests between the quickest worker with logarithms and the quickest calculator operator. Several children also learned to use the slide rule and found interest in working with it in the fourth year (age ten to eleven).

The 'geometry' cards, about sixty in all, began with work on co-ordinates, introduced by chess notation and the game of battle-ships. These involved defining position by numbered squares, for example QP to Q3 in chess, and were, thus, a preliminary to the use of co-ordinates. Simple maps, drawn on a grid of horizontal and vertical numbered lines, followed and the children were asked to give the co-ordinates for specified places and to find the places indicated by given co-ordinates. Compass directions were used in a number of exercises, as in the following example, which increased interest by giving the message in reversed spelling and referring to a map coloured to appear old:

DNATS NO KCALB KCOR DNA ECAF HTRON. HCRAM DRAWROF
YTNEWT EVIF SECAP. NEHT NRUT DNA HCRAM YTRIHT SECAP TSAE
NEHT YTNEWT HTRON NEHT YTROF TSEW NEHT NRUT HTRON
TSAE DNA TA EHT YTRIHT-HTFIF ECAP GID ROF EHT ERUSAERT.
EKAJ

Black Jake hid the treasure on the island. He left these instructions with his map. Can you discover where the treasure is hidden?

Gradually, the maps were made to resemble more and more closely the ordnance survey one inch series and the questions involved not only the reading of co-ordinates but also of contours and the other conventional symbols. The next stage was the introduction of ordnance survey maps with problems involving co-ordinates, road lengths, time taken for journeys at various speeds, planning expeditions and general map reading. As this work proceeded the idea of angles was re-introduced and extended and angles were measured by using a protractor. By the time they were nine, the children were able to do such simple calculations as finding the angles through which the minute hand of a clock turns in specified times or the angles formed by the hour and minute hands at different times. This work also helped to develop a clearer understanding of the use of a magnetic compass.

Practical work with ruler and compasses, such as bisecting angles and constructing different kinds of triangles, was also undertaken and led to exercises like the following:

Take a large sheet of paper and, at the foot, draw a line seven inches long. Mark one end A and the other B. These are two radar stations which are seven miles apart; thus one inch on your scale represents one mile. At the same moment, both stations take a bearing on an aeroplane, C, which is flying past and the interior angle at A is 80° and at B 45°. Draw the triangle making the angles as accurate as possible. How far is the aeroplane from A? How far is the aeroplane from B?

The exercise then gives two other bearings taken a minute later and instructs the child to draw another triangle on the same base and not only to give the new distances from A and B, but also the distance the plane has travelled and its speed. This kind of exercise had a flavour of reality which interested the children. Later, more formal exercises, involving the calculation of angles in given figures with one or two angles known, were used for revision.

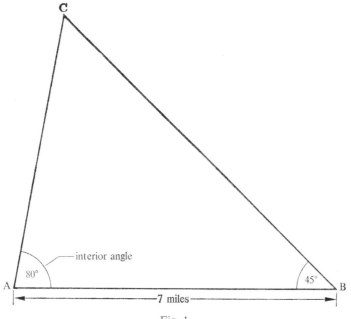

Fig. 1

A number of cards in the series dealt with area and volume, starting with rectangular objects, such as doors and rooms, and going on to objects like tents and cylinders. Towards the end of the series some work with rotations was given, as, for example, in the following exercise, which was accompanied by a diagram of the Plough:

Polaris, the Pole Star, marks the position of the North Pole almost exactly. It is a very important aid to navigation. The position of Polaris is indicated by a group of stars called the Plough, which are part of the constellation Ursa Major or Great Bear. Because the earth is rotating, the stars appear to move across the sky in an anti-clockwise direction. Polaris alone appears to stand still, because it is directly above the northern end of the earth's axis. Since the earth completes one rotation every day, the stars appear to make one complete revolution every twenty-four hours.

On the second sheet of paper you will find a diagram of the Plough as it would appear at 8.00 p.m. on 5 November. Take a similar sheet of graph paper and, using the co-ordinates given, copy the diagram exactly. Do not trace it. Then, remembering that the stars appear to move in an anti-clockwise direction turning through 360° in twenty-four hours, plot as accurately as you can the position of each star in the Plough at 6.00 a.m. on the morning of 6 November. Note down the co-ordinates of each star.

Note: In actual fact the earth makes one complete rotation in 23 hours 56 minutes, so that in twenty-four hours a star would appear to have moved through 361°.

The cards next took up again the concept of co-ordinates and provided exercises in solving equations by using graphs and the series ended with a few cards introducing simple topology.

The children enjoyed working with the cards and they have been referred to in some detail, not because we offer them as models or think them particularly unusual or original, but as examples of the kind of work which clever children of this age group find challenging. They and the topics may be criticized for appearing to be too formal and we, ourselves, felt that the approach might have benefited from being more adventurous. At the same time, we found that the children responded to structured work and that the abler mathematicians among them were happy to deal with concepts surprisingly abstract for their age. The work in the first year was supplemented by the use of 'Geostruct' and 'Polyshape' material; the former being a kit of straws and pipe-cleaners for making three-dimensional shapes and the latter a set of work cards using plastic templates in the construction of three-dimensional geometrical models. The use of teaching machines with a linear programme in mathematics has already been mentioned and the drawback that the programmes often proceeded too slowly for most of the children has been pointed out. One of the boys quickly discovered that he could unscrew part of the cover to enable him to alter incorrect answers. The programmes sometimes contained small inaccuracies which would not normally be noticed, but which a clever child sees at once especially if he has been encouraged at other times to notice anything ambiguous or obscure. At one stage, for example, a programme question read: 'What numbers have you just added together?' and a child wrote '8, 9 and 7' in the window. On turning the knob, he found that the programme's answer was '8 + 9 + 7' and he immediately commented on the mistake, although he tolerantly said 'it's only a minor one'.

By the end of the four years, when the children were eleven, the poorest mathematicians had reached half-way in the two series of cards and the best had gone through them and were doing work normally given to fourteen- or fifteen-year-olds. In addition to the Stillitron programmes already mentioned, the 'Consort mathematics programmes' interested the more advanced children. These children enjoyed working at almost any kind of problem provided it was difficult enough, but they found long routine calculations tedious. So long as the problem offered the right degree of difficulty its challenge would be taken up and enjoyed. Two of the children in the fourth year, for example, surprised us by producing a neat and correctly worked solution to a problem in sets which was much more advanced than would normally be considered appropriate for their age. On being asked where they found the problem they produced an examination paper they had come across which had been set at ordinary level in the General Certificate of Education and was, therefore, suitable for children who had spent four or five years in a secondary school and who were five or six years older than they. The problem had interested them so they combined to solve it.

Progress at this rate in the primary school must inevitably lead to problems in the secondary school unless provision is also made there for children to work at their own pace. If clever children are to be interested and happy in their work, it must be difficult enough to challenge them and, generally speaking, in mathematics this means acceleration, particularly for the abler mathematicians among them. When the concept or process which is the basis of one set of problems is understood and used easily, its challenge has been overcome and, if the ability of the mathematically minded clever child is to be catered for, he must meet other concepts and other processes. Thus, by the time he is eleven years old, he will be working at the level of, say, the fourteen- or fifteen-year-old and he may lose interest if, on passing to the secondary school, he finds himself repeating the kind of work he has already done. If, however, education is to suit the abilities and aptitudes of each child, it is indefensible to avoid this difficulty by holding a mathematically clever child back in the primary school by making him continue working on problems he can already do. The solution must be found in closer consultation between secondary and primary teachers so that his secondary programme is designed to follow smoothly on the work he has done according to his ability.

Imaginative work

5

Reading

It would be unusual for a child of IQ 130 or above, brought up in normal circumstances, to face his teacher with reading difficulties at the age of seven. It is far more likely that his reading age will be two or more years in advance of his chronological age and that he will happily pick up and read books which interest him. The teacher's problem with these children, then, is not in teaching them how to read, but in stimulating and widening their interests in reading so as to strengthen it as a habit and to develop their discrimination as readers. By the time they leave the infant school, some of them will already be reading books from a public library, not all of which will be children's books. For others, comics, magazines and parts of the daily newspaper will be the staple diet. Much will depend on the reading habits of their families and friends and the kind of reading material available in school. It is clear that the ample provision of a wide variety of books in school and class libraries is essential and the children must have free access to them. Records of what our children read at home and in school during their four years in the class do not, in general, show any sustained preferences for particular kinds of material, although there are one or two possible exceptions to this. The reading of comics persisted throughout the period and titles such as *Dandy* and *Beano* appear in the fourth, as well as in the first, year. They do not, however, seem to have formed an important part of most children's reading, which was fairly wide in scope. At one time in the first year, for example, one eight-year-old boy was reading, in addition to comics, *The Hobbit* and a book about the microscope and how to use it. Another boy's reading ranged from children's annuals to books on chess, archery, stamp collecting, birds and the seashore. Paddington the bear, and Dr Dolittle were among the favourite characters, particularly for the boys, but, at

F

the same time, stories of historical characters such as Captain Scott, Henry V, Marco Polo and Captain Cook were read with enjoyment. One book, *The Bowmen of Creçy* was very popular with the boys and inspired several attempts at bow making. At the age of eight, one of the less communicative boys was reading about magnets and batteries, the weather, air and flight, animals, the seashore, life before man, Roman Britain and Robert the Bruce. This boy's reading was an exception to the general pattern of indiscriminate choice in showing a persistent bias, at first towards stories of well known figures, usually warriors or explorers, and later to accounts of battles and military campaigns. Throughout the four years, the girls' reading was generally less wide and a good deal of it was taken up with school stories or, in the earlier years, with stories of fairies and witches. Two or three of the girls were voracious readers and, in general, the girls read more than the boys. Classroom provision played a large part in determining what was read both in school and at home and there was some tendency for friends to read the same books. Interest in certain authors, for example Tolkien, sprang from the teacher's reading aloud from their books.

Our experience, then, with these clever children confirmed the importance, for them as for other children, of paying careful attention not only to the number, but also to the kind, of books provided in the school or class library. What children read is, to a large extent, determined by what is readily available and this appears to be as true for the highly intelligent seven- to eleven-year-old as it is for others of the same age. A child will take from the shelves an attractively presented book, particularly with interesting illustrations, and if he enjoys reading it, he will come back for another by the same author or for another of what appears to him to be the same kind of book. At this age, it is important to establish firmly the habit of reading and this is best done through enjoyment. A bright child, like any other, may find, from time to time, that he has made a mistake and that he does not like the book he has chosen. There is no virtue in trying to make him persevere; he should feel free to return it, unfinished, to the shelves without any adverse comment. His teacher will have found herself, from time to time, unable ot read a particular book or another and there is no reason to expect the child to be different. Freedom of this kind is important if the development of a child's taste and discrimination in reading is to be fostered without giving him a distaste for literature.

Records of what our children read show the importance of providing a wide range not only of fiction but also of non-fiction, such as stories from history and bigrography, books on hobbies, everyday things, nature, animals, elementary science and other countries. These need not be written for children so long as they are interesting in theme and readable in style. By the age of eleven, our children were enjoying having read to them passages from such books as *The War of the Worlds,* and *The Diary of a Fox Hunting Man* and among the books they were reading were *The Lord of the Rings, Three Men in a Boat, The Early Churchills* and some simple science fiction.

It is important to have a good and attractive encyclopaedia readily accessible. Through the generosity of Field Enterprises Educational Corporation our children were fortunate in having *The World Book Encyclopaedia* in their classroom. Although an adult publication, this encyclopaedia had an immediate appeal because it is most attractively presented and lavishly illustrated, very often in colour. The language used and the arrangement of information in the articles are aimed at ease of understanding and several of our children would read long articles in it for pleasure. They soon learned how to find the right volume and look up the topic they wanted and they were helped in this by the exercises in finding information described in chapter 3.

It seems, to us, unwise to expect even a clever child of this age group to write a report, however, short, on each book read. Writing is notoriously more arduous than reading or speaking, even for adults, and young children can find its difficulties frustrating. The clever child who can read quickly may be tempted to limit his reading if he has to write a report on each book, and his pleasure in reading may be overcome by his aversion to writing. The teacher can extend the range of interest, not only by reading aloud from different books, but also by encouraging and stimulating informal discussion of what the children are reading. Here again, it would seem that the emphasis should be on informality. The children, too, may like to read aloud, to their companions or the teacher, passages they find particularly striking in books they enjoy. Telling a story to a group of clever children can be a trying experience because it often happens that the more interested they become, the more they want to ask questions, until the thread of the story is lost. At times a dramatic dénouement is reached, only to be completely spoiled by a particularly imaginative child leaping to the solution and announcing it with a broad grin on his face.

Story-telling

Many clever children, although not all, will surprise a teacher, first meeting them at the age of seven, by their facility in writing. Although insecure at times, spelling is generally good and sentences are ably constructed. Conversation may be invented and written with correct punctuation. Some children, between seven and eight, will write stories twenty or thirty pages long, divided into chapters, with a table of contents and illustrations. Talent of this kind has to be stimulated and encouraged and this is particularly important for the highly divergent thinkers. Convergent thinkers, too, who delight in solving problems in mathematics and logical reasoning need to be encouraged to exercise their imaginations in a free-ranging way. A starter is all that is needed to set their imaginations to work and give them a possible direction. For this purpose, we devised a series of some 160 'Just imagine' cards. Unlike the other cards we used, this series did not present a graded sequence and, although some cards were, perhaps, more complicated than others, there was no correct order and a child could choose any card which appealed to him. This is not to say that he was given the whole set to choose from each time. Every teacher knows that young children, even the clever ones, can be as frustrated by too much choice as by too little. Where there are too many alternatives, the difficulty of making up one's mind can be agonizing. We found it best to let our eight- or nine-year-olds choose a card from five to ten possibilities. Later, a child might ask for a card from a particular group, say one about the sea or about space travel, and he was then given the cards in that group from which to make his choice.

Each card began with a picture, drawn and coloured by the teacher, followed by some information aimed at stimulating imaginative writing. One group presented straightforward dramatic situations, such as a flood, a sinking ship and an unexpected holiday; another was concerned with escapes and brought forth a good deal of ingenuity. A number of cards suggested pursuit stories which involved reference to an atlas and sometimes to an airline timetable. One card, which was popular with boys and girls in the first year, depicted a large black spider, told the child that he had just opened a shop to sell spiders and asked him to write an advertisement or paragraph for publication which would persuade people to come and buy them. In all these cards the illustrations were of prime importance and the information only secondary in capturing the initial interest of young children. They were simple, in colour, and conventional in representation, all characteristics which appealed to our children and their effectiveness appeared to be increased by their having been drawn for them by the teacher.

As one would expect, the children's responses to the cards varied widely, not only in quality, length and style, but also in form. While the usual response was the writing of a story or verse, a series of illustrations linked by short sentences or even an attempt at a short play were offered from time to time. A child might turn a serious subject into comedy or give a comic one serious treatment. In the first year, for example, a seven-year-old boy chose a card about a journey in a balloon and produced four drawings of a balloon, each one smaller than the preceding one. When asked what this meant, he said, 'The balloon is getting higher and higher, and after a month they are so high up they meet God.' This event was to be the subject of his fifth illustration. This boy later produced some lively long stories, always with a strong visual element; whole episodes being compressed into a few sentences and a graphic illustration. Some of the children, from the second year onwards, showed a preference for cards suggesting stories which needed a good deal of background information. Three boys who wrote stories about an air race in 1912 spent a long time looking up details of aircraft of that time so that their stories would be as accurate as possible. One of the girls, on the other hand, who decided that the heroine of her story should be involved in an attempted kidnapping in a park in San Francisco, examined a plan of the city but, finding that none of the parks shown would suit her, invented one that fitted her purpose. A boy who chose to make up a historical story wanted a lot of information about British infantry regiments and the composition and tactics of an infantry battalion. He involved the teacher in a detailed discussion of a defensive battle to hold a river bridge and went to the length of using an ordance survey map to choose his position. He then had a long discussion with the teacher about the probable outcome of the battle, taking into consideration the nature of the terrain, the effect of surprise, musketry and mortar fire. Even one of the girls, who was usually careless about detail, examined a plan of an ocean liner to find out the position of the cabins before she wrote a story about a shipwreck.

As time went on, some of the children were confident enough to want to try out ideas of their own and they were encouraged to make cards and write about them. When a child finished a card the other children discussed it and decided whether or not it should be added to the series. A child who did not want to write a card would often suggest ideas for cards to the teacher and the teacher also wrote cards to meet special requests, for example, from a child who liked writing stories about boarding schools and another who wanted to write about a scout troop. It is interesting to notice that even those children who had a general theme in mind wanted a card to start them off on a story. Stories suggested by the same card were widely different, but it seemed as if the initial suggestion was needed to release the child's invention.

Some children enjoyed reading their stories to the others and sometimes an interesting discussion would develop afterwards. From time to time, children would tell their stories to a tape recorder. One girl, for example, who was highly imaginative and verbal, complained that, no matter how quickly she wrote, she could not keep up with the ideas crowding before her and she often forgot the best ones before she could get them down. Once she had mastered its use, she found the tape recorder a welcome solution to her difficulty. This child was also a keen young actress and, in dictating her stories, she found scope for this talent, giving each of her characters a distinctive voice and accent and wringing every ounce of drama out of the story.

Every teacher of English knows that knowing when and how to criticize a pupil's original writing is crucial in its development. It has already been mentioned that, from our observation, clever children will probably have a fair grasp of syntax and punctuation by the age of seven, although spelling might be comparatively weak, even in an avid reader. Nevertheless, mistakes will occur, and there may be serious lapses in sentence construction and punctuation, especially in long stories or when ideas are too plentiful to be controlled. In our experience, it was not uncommon for stories to run to several chapters and for the writing to become breathless when exciting incidents were portrayed. In these circumstances there seems to be no rule that the teacher as critic can follow, except that nothing must be said or done to inhibit the urge to write. Moreover, a clever child usually knows exactly what he wants to say and is well aware of any failure to say it. Added to his self criticism, his teacher's adverse comments can bear much more heavily on him than was intended and serve only to discourage further writing. Much will depend on the child's temperament and the teacher's sensitivity to it, and whether or not the criticism is offered in the form of friendly help. One final point, to be emphasized again, is that not all clever children have a talent for imaginative writing; those, for example, whose talents are spatial-constructional and not verbal may be genuinely distressed by any attempt on the part of the teacher to make them spend time on work of this kind and they are, then, likely to react by being stubbornly resistant to it. If, however, they are compelled to write, the result is unlikely to be worth either their effort or that of the teacher.

Poetry and drama

Every parent knows that verse with marked rhyme and rhythm has a strong appeal for young children and ours, when they came to us, were no different in this respect from other seven-year-olds. There was no need to persuade them to enjoy verse; all that was necessary was to widen their enjoyment to include as wide a variety of forms and themes as possible. Poetry is to be heard, and this is specially true for children whose experience of it is limited. Plenty of opportunity was, therefore, provided for speaking and reading poetry aloud. This is one of the many normal class activities in which the clever child will be able to join. During the first two years, the teacher read a lot of poetry to the children, who would repeat and very readily memorize poems and passages which particularly appealed to them. They talked about the poems and many of them enjoyed writing verses of their own. The following is an example from a nine-year-old girl:

> *Midnight*
> The clock strikes twelve,
> All is quiet except for the
> Oohing of the tired old owl,
> And the noisey noise of a

Train as it passes
Taking your letters or bringing
them back.

The poem is reproduced just as it was written and, needless to say, no notice was taken of the spelling mistake. No pressure of any kind was put on the children to write verse; those who wanted to do so were encouraged and reluctance on the part of others was accepted. Interest in verse writing had waned by the third year, when the children were ten, but choral speaking had become very popular. It is difficult to suggest reasons for this change of emphasis, but one part of the explanation may be that, as their insight into the poet's meaning developed, the children became increasingly interested in the challenge of conveying it in spoken sound. At the same time they were becoming increasingly aware of the possibilities in choral speaking. However this may be, their interest provided excellent opportunities for developing critical awareness through the discussion of how different lines might be most effectively spoken. In the fourth year the emphasis changed again; this time to the more private, individual choice and enjoyment of poetry. By then, one or two boys, who had not hitherto shown much interest in poetry, found themselves enjoying some, often heroic, poems. It looked as if, given time and freedom from pressure, even those who were indifferent to poetry might acquire a taste for some of it. Throughout the four years, poetry activities were varied and informal. Sometimes a child would bring a poem he had found to the teacher for discussion; at others informal groups of two or three children would read favourite verse together, or make little programmes of poetry reading and record them on tape.

In common with most young children, those in our group already liked to act when they came to us. Miming and the acting of incidents made up on the spur of the moment were popular. Most successful were incidents providing plenty of simple dramatic action and a part for everyone. Towards the third year, character acting became possible and a particularly popular game was one in which the children took it in turns to portray different characters, while the others tried to guess the characters portrayed. At times, groups of three or four children would improvise scenes showing a particular quality or emotion, such as joy, fear, anger, courage. Dramatic activities in the fourth year became more ambitious. One which persisted over a considerable period of time was the making of a film. This introduced the possibilities of film editing and offered scope particularly appreciated by a high spatial-divergent thinker. Similar scope was also offered in the recording of a play on tape. This boy and two or three others were particularly interested in the technicalities of making a sound-play. They became responsible for choosing and recording incidental music and appropriate sound effects, while others read the play. The synchronizing of the sound effects was one of the interesting problems facing them in this activity.

Reading aloud, choral speaking, miming and acting provide plenty of opportunity for group and class activities in which the clever child can and should take part. He experiences the satisfaction of contributing to a co-operative enterprise, the success of which is the achievement of each one engaged in it, and it will also be good for him to find that other children, not as clever as he is, may be better actors.

Music

Music is another important activity in providing for imaginative development, but it must not be assumed that clever children will be musically gifted. The musical ability of our children, for example, as tested by the Wing test (Wing, 1968), covered the range one would expect to find in any class of young children of normal intelligence. In our group, the scores of five children were in grade A, four in grade B and six in grade C. We found, however, that the performance of these children in music, as in art and craft, benefited from their general intellectual competence and good hand and eye co-ordination.

Individual work

Some of the work done by the children was individual, listening to a tape recording and following directions and answering questions from a work card. To do this a child would go into another room alone, but if no other room had been available, it would have been possible for him to work, using headphones, in the classroom. It is easy to see that if a language laboratory is available, good use of it can be made for this purpose. Working individually seemed to be particularly suitable for such tasks as picking out different instruments, or identifying and recording points of dynamic interest or ·

phrasing in an orchestral piece. The record 'The instruments of the orchestra', introduced by Yehudi Menuhin, is a useful starting point and a child can be asked to write the name of each instrument and something about its sound which will help him to remember it. Our children, later, went on to listen to concertos for particular instruments and excerpts featuring a particular instrument from other works, such as the cor anglais in Berlioz, 'Roman Carnival' overture. Recognizing recurrent themes and rhythms followed. Lists of suitable records are to be found in Dobbs (1966) and Dwyer (1967). Dictation from a specially prepared tape recording was also suitable for individual work after the children, as a group, had been introduced to writing single notes and simple sequences of notes as they heard them played. They appeared to be interested in acquiring this skill, but it is probably more suitable for the highly intelligent than for the less able.

There was a good deal of interest in different instruments and the sounds produced by them, an interest which was strengthened by visits of individual musicians who came to demonstrate and talk about their instruments. On one occasion, the children went to a local church for a lecture-demonstration on the organ. In addition to the interest of the demonstrations themselves, they stimulated a few children to undertake quite sizeable studies of particular instruments. One boy, for example, was fascinated by the working of the organ and spent many hours drawing sketches, describing how it worked, the effects of using different manuals and stops and how these effects were produced. Ready access to standard works of reference is essential for projects of this kind.

Individual tuition on piano or guitar was given to any child who showed an interest in it and, as might be expected, progress and aptitude were related more to his musical ability, as measured by the Wing test, than to his IQ or level of divergent thinking. General intellectual ability appeared to play an important part in such matters as the mastery of notation in piano playing and the recognition and translation of chord symbols into hand shapes for the guitar. For playing both these instruments, however, physical muscular control and co-ordination appear to be crucial and the highly intelligent child does not necessarily have an aptitude for the finer movements and skills required for the development of a good technique.

Some attempt was made, not very successfully, to interest the children in making simple instruments. Our experience suggests that success in this depends to some extent on the children's other experience in craft. If children become absorbed, as most of ours did, in various craft projects which fully occupy the time available, they will be reluctant to find time for another project unless its interest is more compelling than that of the one it replaces. The effect on instrument making of enthusiasm for craft work can, thus, in some circumstances, be as unfortunate as indifference to it. Useful suggestions for making simple instruments are to be found in Roberts (1969), and Williams (1971).

Improvisation

The greater part of our children's musical activities took the form of improvisation, which was a particular interest of the teacher and had the advantage of being an experience they had not previously encountered in school. Improvisation was mainly a group activity for which pitch-percussion instruments of the Orff type were used: xylophone, metallophone and glockenspiel, all with removable bars; drum and chime bars of the independent free-standing type so as to be easily divided among the group; tambourines, castanets, triangles and cymbals. These instruments were chosen because they require little technique to play and are likely to encourage more confident playing than are instruments, like the piano and recorder, which require a high degree of control and discrimination in playing. Children are often discouraged from improvising by lack of technical confidence and by confusion caused by the wide range of notes available on an instrument. Thus, by providing instruments which only needed to be struck, and reducing confusion by providing only the notes of the pentatonic scale, the children were helped to gain confidence from the beginning, and their enthusiasm grew as they found their efforts satisfying.

In our experience, four appeared to be the most satisfactory number for a group. At first, most of the children appeared to have no interest in the contributions of other members of their group and some would even attempt to wander away if they were not playing a main part. Nevertheless, we thought it valuable to insist on group work, not only for the beneficial experience of working together, but also because ensemble playing tends to encourage more fluent and less hesitant improvisation. A beginning was made with two notes, C and E, and only these were placed on the xylophone. A child was then encouraged to make up a tune using the two notes while the rest of the group beat a simple rhythmic accompaniment on drum, castanets and tambourine. This procedure was followed as each new note was added: the fifth (C, E, G), then the sixth (C, E, G, A) and, finally, the second (C, D, E, G, A), thus completing the pentatonic scale. When the children were improvising fluently and confidently in this way, the ideas of a ground bass, a sustained pedal base and a chord basis were introduced and the glockenspiel, chime bars and metallophone brought into use. The use of the pentatonic scale ensured that there were no problems of discord or clash of harmonies, but progress to work in major and minor keys would be possible with children of this age if they were musically talented and able to grasp the concepts of tonality and harmony involved. Our children went on to set to music verses of poems they were reading; each member of a group, in turn, providing one line and the others discussing its merits and suitability before accepting it and writing it down. This activity provided the teacher with the opportunity of introducing very simple ideas of binary and ternary form.

Improvisations the children wanted to keep were often tape recorded, but some, especially group settings of verses, were written down. The general intellectual ability of these children appeared to be helpful here, because they were more able than is usual at their age to remember the notes they had played and, thus to repeat a tune they had improvised. Once they were familiar with the idea of improvising in groups, the children were also able to work individually with the instrument and in the style of improvisation which they preferred. A supporting activity, throughout, was the development of rhythmic sense through a game which was much enjoyed and was often played at the beginning of an improvisation session. To play the game, the children formed a circle. The 'beat' was counted for them in two-bar units either of three beats, or four beats, in a bar. Each child, in turn, claps a rhythmical series to the beat, extending over the two-bar unit and this series is then repeated by the whole group. Children are 'out' if they repeat a rhythm which has already been clapped, or if they break the constancy of the beat.

Singing, listening and group projects

Singing was not overlooked and much use was made of folk songs with guitar accompaniments. Instrumental parts, too, would often be provided by the children. Part-singing was begun at the age of about eight, as is quite common with children of this age. Listening to music was also attempted, although with difficulty, because the lively and active dispositions of the children made it difficult for them to adapt to the apparently passive role of listeners. The reasons for this are not by any means clear and it would be unwise to attribute it to the level and kind of the children's intelligence. However, it was thought desirable to persevere with listening, giving the children guide-lines and points to listen for, as a necessary part of musical education. By the time they reached the age of eleven, there were only two children who consistently found it almost impossible to concentrate on listening to music. Finally, a number of group projects were undertaken. A topic such as the sea or summer would be chosen and the children collected factual information, stories, pictures and poems, including their own compositions, on the topic. They then improvised appropriate 'mood' music, or settings of verses, and presented the collected work to another group of children. Similarly, a more ambitious project took the form of music and drama. The children would make up a short sketch of an incident in some well-known story, writing the dialogue and making the scenery and improvising tunes to represent and accompany the characters. Looking back, the most valuable activities with these particular children seemed to be the work in improvisation and the group activities.

Some books for music teaching

Teachers may be interested in a list of books we found useful. It is divided into rough categories for convenience.

Instrument making

Roberts, R. (1969), *Musical Instruments Made to be Played*, Dryad Press, London.
Williams, P. H. M. (1971), *Lively Craft Cards, Set 2, Making Musical Instruments*, Mills & Boon, London.

Singing

Brocklehurst, B. (1968), *Pentatonic Song Book*, Schott, London.

Chatterley, A. (1969), *Seventy Simple Songs with ostinati*, Novello, London.

Noble, R. (1967), *Three Chords and Beyond*, Novello, London.

Music projects

Addison, R. (1967), *Children make Music*, Holmes-McDougall, London.

Dennis, B. (1970), *Experimental Music in Schools*, Oxford University Press.

Horton, J. (1969), *The Music Group*, Schott, London.

John, M. (ed.), (1971), *Music Drama in Schools*, Cambridge University Press.

Lawrence, I. (1967), *Projects in Music*, Longman, London.

Paynter, J. and Aston, P. (1970), *Sound and Silence*, Cambridge University Press.

Classroom reference books

Larousse Encyclopaedia of Music (1971), Hamlyn, London.

Scholes, Percy A. (1955), *The Listener's History of Music*, Oxford University Press.

Scholes, Percy A. (1968), *The Concise Oxford Dictionary of Music*, Oxford University Press.

Scholes, Percy A. (1970), *The Oxford Companion to Music*, Oxford University Press.

Winters, G. (1967), *Musical Instruments in the Classroom*, Longman, London.

General

Brocklehurst, B. (1971), *Response to Music*, Routledge & Kegan Paul, London.

Dobbs, J. P. B. (1966), *The Slow Learner and Music*, Oxford University Press.

Dwyer, T. (1967), *Teaching Musical Appreciation*, Oxford University Press.

Dwyer, T. (1971), *Composing with Tape Recorders*, Oxford University Press.

Evans, K. (1971), *Creative Singing*, Oxford University Press.

Garnett, H. (1971), *Practical Music Making with Juniors*, Schoolmaster Publishing Co., London.

Pape, M. (1970), *Growing up with Music*, Oxford University Press.

Swanwick K. (1968), *Popular Music and the Teacher*, Pergamon, London.

Miscellaneous activities

6

Second language: German

It is common, nowadays, for children to begin learning a second language in school when they are about eight years old. This is, perhaps, particularly important for clever children because it provides them with a new and challenging activity and enriches the curriculum for them. Some of them, too, are likely to make exceptionally good progress in the language in these early years. The second language usually begun at this age in English schools is French, but for our children it was German. It is generally agreed that the approach to the new language should be through speech and it is important that the teacher should be able to speak it well and fluently. Our children were fortunate in having a native German teacher who had taught in Germany and in England and who was able to introduce them to German life and manners from her own experience. In the first year the teacher was able to visit the class for half an hour each day, an arrangement which seemed particularly suitable for these young beginners. In the two succeeding years a daily visit was not possible and three periods of one hour each were substituted. The result of the change did not prove in any way unsatisfactory as the children, being older and already beginning to feel more at home with the language, were able to take the longer periods and the intervals between them in their stride. As time went on, it became not uncommon for some of the children to intersperse snatches of German in their ordinary conversation and the class teacher, too, was able to help them to keep in practice. The aim was to enable them to speak as much simple, everyday German as possible, in a meaningful way, with acceptable intonation and pronunciation, and to gain some facility in reading.

As was usual with these children, the lessons had to be free; the teacher soon found that making them follow a strictly planned route for any length of time was ineffective in terms of the amount of German learned. They did not respond to attempts to teach them in the continuous, strict, thorough way which the teacher had experienced, both as pupil and teacher, in Germany. No doubt the ineffectiveness of this method sprang, partly at least, from the assertiveness of their own interests and ideas and the generally free approach to other parts of the curriculum. Two examples of the kinds of lessons to which they responded might be given. One came immediately after the mid-day recess for lunch, during which the teacher had done some shopping. On arriving in the classroom, she would let a child unpack her shopping bag and name each article or ask the others to do so. Then two children might act a scene as shopkeeper and customer and it was not long before they would punctuate their normal shopping conversation by humorous remarks, not always in correct German, which showed that they were beginning to feel at home with the language. A period of reading and questioning would follow, often interrupted by other questions and remarks by the children. Finally, if there were time, a song or two might be sung, but in the last year this was not enjoyed much by some of the boys who regarded it as a little childish and girlish. Another lesson might begin with the checking of the understanding of something previously read, with one of the children acting as the teacher. The reading of a dramatic scene would follow, with different children reading different parts. Their love of acting led them to writing their own scenes, which included, for example, some lively ones at the doctor's and the dentist's. They were critical of one another's performances and particularly severe on over-acting

Grammar as such was avoided, but familiarity with such matters as changes in word endings and conjugation was gained through different kinds of games. For at least the first half of the course, the work was oral and, as far as possible, in German. Writing was generally postponed until the final year, and translation was done very rarely. The children readily asked for an explanation of anything they did not understand. During the final year, after the children had had more than two years' oral German, we were interested to find that, although most of them understood very well and could use the language correctly, they could not translate well into English. One would say 'I know what it means but I can't say it in English; it sounds wrong.' This was, of course, because they were trying to translate more or less literally and they might puzzle for ten minutes

G

or so before some of them hit on the corresponding idiomatic
English. Apparently, as a result of our determination that they
should learn the new language as naturally as possible, they were
able to express themselves in English or in German, but the two
languages were quite separate and they could not easily move from
the one to the other. In so far as this meant that they were not
thinking in English and then translating into German before speaking, it was encouraging; translating as an art could be practised
later.

As one might expect, progress varied considerably in the group.
Differences, which were hardly noticeable during the first year of the
course, became very marked in the last. Six or seven children showed
a real talent for the language, two or three were neither good nor
particularly interested and the others were quite good. In some
instances, the children's ability could adversely affect their performance. A clever child, full of ideas which he is able to express
freely in his mother tongue, can find the limitations imposed on him
as a beginner in a new language frustrating and discouraging and,
unless strongly motivated, he can become bored and give up. He
may also be handicapped by his impatience to get on quickly
increasing his unwillingness to undertake essential repetitive
learning.

Art and craft

A clever child, like any other, usually enjoys working with his hands,
especially if he is given the opportunity to choose his own task. We
found it best to provide as wide a diversity of materials as possible
and to allow the children to draw, paint, or make models as they
chose. The teacher's function was to be at hand to give guidance,
suggestions and help whenever necessary. The materials provided
were those normally available in most classrooms for children of
seven to eleven and included balsa wood, card, sugar paper, tissue
paper, polystyrene foam sheets and balls, soft wire, pipe cleaners,
straws, sticks, clay, plasticine, coloured paper, metal foil paper,
cardboard boxes, bobbins, wooden wheels and dowelling, plaster
bandage, powder paint, wax crayons, coloured pencils, felt pens,
adhesives such as Copydex and balsa glue, assorted card, plastic
bottles and boxes.

Sometimes, a child would work on his own; at others, several children or even the whole group would work together on a large project which, in the first year, was often prompted by a particular occasion. It was noticeable that some children, particularly the more divergent thinkers, were never satisfied with what had been done, but were continually thinking of 'improvements' which involved such continual reconstruction that the project was destroyed. For their first Christmas in the class, for example, when they were eight years old, some of the boys built a good nativity scene, complete with plasticine models of Jesus, Mary, Joseph and the shepherds. Then came the 'improvements'; the shepherds had to be made more realistic; Joseph needed a lantern that would light, with the wires buried in his coat, and so on until the whole model was destroyed.

In the second year, a boy of eight made a very good model yacht from a piece of balsa wood which he had shaped, with dowelling for a mast, and white paper sails. He mounted the model on a wooden base, covered with blue tissue paper to represent the sea. He did not, however, allow it to remain on show in the classroom very long before he took it apart, gouged a recess in the hull into which he fitted an electric motor, connected to it a propeller from a model aeroplane and added a battery. He now had a model motor boat which actually worked, although much to his amusement, it went backwards until he changed the wiring. At a later stage, the same piece of wood became the body of a model car.

During the third year, the children increasingly wanted to use the time given to art and craft to work on illustrations or models connected with their particular interests. A demand grew up for designs to help them and, in response to it, the teacher embarked on the production of various craft books. These included books of ship and aircraft plans and armour and costume books, containing directions for making cut-out figures which could be dressed and suitably coloured and mounted on a sheet of paper as a display, or made free-standing, as figures in a tableau. Connections with other work being done were exploited; thus the aircraft plans formed part of a work book on flight which contained directions for simple scientific experiments in aerodynamics as well as plans for model making. The book of ships became so popular that all the children joined in building a sizeable fleet. On another occasion, after seeing the film of *Henry V*, they made a model of the battle of Agincourt. A good deal of work in art and craft was also done in connection with film making.

It is quite possible that a teacher will find that the one or two clever children in her class are not artistically gifted, but their contribution is likely to be valuable because it displays one or more of the following qualities to a greater degree than usual: imagination, sensitivity, painstaking accuracy, intelligent and confident handling of materials. The unusual ideas, or high constructional ability, of one of these children can be very much appreciated by the others in a class when they are intent on working out a common project, and the more opportunities a clever child has of experiencing satisfaction by using his abilities in the common service, the better.

Physical education and games

It is by now well known that the idea that clever children are well below the average for their age in physique is totally misconceived and is nothing more than a figment of the popular imagination. The fact is, as Terman and others have long since shown, that the advantage lies in the opposite direction; clever children tend to be taller and heavier than other children of the same age. An examination of the children in our group provides an interesting illustration although the numbers involved were too small for any firm conclusions to be drawn from the tests. Six tests of physical ability were given to our children when they were nine and to two other groups of the same age, in the normal intelligence range. These latter groups were matched with ours in sex and for the socio-economic class of the fathers. Both groups were from the same city: one from a 'down-town' school, and the other from a school serving a select residential suburb. Four of the tests, for double hand grip, standing broad jump, agility run and balance walk had been widely used before; two, namely, throw and catch and alternate hop were devised for this occasion. A study of the results showed that, in general, it could be said that the more intelligent children showed, over-all, the greater ability in dynamic activities involving basic physical qualities such as strength and speed. A comparison of the performance of our group with that of the other two groups combined, in double-hand grip, standing broad jump and agility run, gave significant figures in favour of our group for all three tests, two of them at the 1 per cent level of confidence. In activities in which performance is determined more by factors other than the basic physical qualities such as strength and speed, there were differences in performance between the groups, but no coherent pattern to them. Any tendency which appeared to exist was again in favour of the more intelligent children. It is also interesting to note that the testers, who had not previously met any of the children, found our group of clever children the most difficult to test because they continually asked the reasons for various instructions and invented possible situations in which the instructions might be ambiguous, or only applicable with difficulty, or even absurd. The children in the other groups generally accepted the instructions and followed them without question.

Our children, generally, showed little interest in the small individual activities usual in physical education for young children, but were happiest when they could devise activities on large apparatus such as the climbing frame and box or on a large mat. A short time, usually about half an hour, was devoted to physical education each day and, for these children, acted as a very desirable safety valve. In general the girls were not quite as enthusiastic about physical education as the boys, but some of them were quite good performers, and one, very graceful. As the group was small in number, it was possible to have as few as three children using one piece of apparatus at a time. It was, however, necessary for the teacher to be constantly aware of the use being made of each piece of apparatus by the groups into which the class had been divided because of the marked tendency, particularly on the part of some children, to invent activities which could be dangerous.

Games of all kinds were popular and some of the boys at nine and ten years old developed such an obsession for association football that they talked and wrote of little else. By the fourth year, some of this enthusiasm was waning, but those who were in the school team remained as keen as ever. Those who were really committed to the game brought to it the same single-minded purpose and energy that they brought to any chosen activity and they would organize training sessions, discuss tactics, and analyse their mistakes after a match. The girls, too, enjoyed games and some of them were in the school netball team in the fourth year, but they were never as enthusiastic as the boys. Basket ball was played in some physical education periods in the fourth year and all the children were able to swim by the end of that year. In general, it may be said that they shared the liking of normal healthy children of their age for physical education and games and that their intelligence helped them to make full use of whatever skill they had.

Visits

The educational value of properly prepared visits for all children has long been generally accepted and for clever children such visits provide a valuable means of enriching the curriculum. Not only do they take the children out of school, but they often enable them to meet experts and hear them talk about their own specialisms. Some visits, such as those to the seashore, the countryside, parks or around the neighbourhood of the school, are a means of direct learning through observing, handling and collecting, under the guidance of the class teacher. Our children, for example, at an early age, enjoyed collecting objects systematically from the beach and bringing them back to school and identifying and classifying them. For a clever child, a problem in identification can provide the thrill of a detective investigation with its clues to be followed and theories to be tested and discarded until the mystery is solved. Subsequently, classification and display give him the opportunity to exercise his orderly, methodical skill and his imagination in making his arrangement attractive. Opportunities are also given for individuals to write or speak about their collections.

Clever children, too, because of their intellectual ability, are able to take very full advantage of any special facilities to which they may have access. On one occasion, for example, when they were about eight years old, our children were taken to the university where the Professor of Egyptology let them see and handle objects in the museum and explained many of the ideas and customs of ancient Egypt. The children's close observation of details, even before they were pointed out, was shown by the questions they asked, and their later written work and discussion showed what a valuable experience this had been for them. This visit, and one to the city museum to study early man, were made when prehistoric man and early civilizations were topics in the curriculum. The museum visit, one of the earliest when the children were aged seven, emphasized the need to reconcile freedom and direction discussed in an earlier chapter. It was probably made too early, before the children had fully settled down in their new class. It did, however, provide examples of unusual thinking, such as that of one boy who was found trying various stone hand axes and scrapers, first in one hand then in the other, to see whether they fitted a right- or left-handed man. At a later stage, visits to a planetarium and a radio-telescope coincided with a programme about the universe and one to an air training station was related to a science programme on flight. The children were allowed to sit in the cockpit of a chipmunk trainer and to look inside a jet engine. Field trips to the shore and local parks were made in connection with curriculum topics and a five-day holiday in the Lake District towards the end of the fourth year provided opportunities for practical geography, geology and biology which were very much enjoyed. A visit which produced some of the best quality written work in science was that to the rural studies centre of a college of education. The children found the wide variety of animal and plant life available for study most stimulating and they gained much from having individual tuition from student-teachers who were specializing in the subject. The student-teachers found the children's questions interesting and were often caught unawares by their quality. Other visits, for example to see historical films, were made; the ones above are mentioned simply to illustrate some of the uses made of local possibilities. It would seem that while curriculum enrichment of this kind is valuable for all children, it is, perhaps, a necessity in the education of the clever child in the normal class.

It has already been noticed that an important contribution to enrichment provided by certain visits is the opportunity for children to hear experts talking about their own subjects. This, too, seems to be particularly rewarding with clever children, no matter whether a visit is involved or the expert comes to school to talk to the class. If the visitor is prepared to talk in a straightforward and clear way and is ready to answer questions and discuss points with children, the response can be most rewarding. A clever child's own ability enables him to recognize and appreciate expert knowledge and skill and direct contact with it helps to make real to him standards of excellence which he is already interested in achieving.

Our experience, therefore, suggests that an invaluable way of enriching the curriculum and providing for the abilities of clever children, scattered over a number of schools and classes, is to bring them together for, say, one day each week in a centre possessing specialists and facilities not available in their own schools. A college of education can provide a very good centre, as Bridges and his colleagues showed at Brentwood. The activities at the centre must not be looked upon as the icing on a cake, but as an integral part of each child's curriculum and must be planned with his particular abilities and needs in mind. This planning will necessitate close consultation between centre staff and the children's class teachers, a process which will benefit not only the children, but also those taking part in it. The possibilities are wide and can be far-reaching and arrangements of this kind are being made in a growing number of places. Through them, the challenge needed by clever children for the full development of their abilities can be provided, without the social and personal disadvantages which would result from their separate education.

Further reading

7

Ever since Terman began his studies of the gifted there has been a growing volume of papers and books in English on the subject, especially in the USA where much of the work relates to pupils aged twelve and above. It is, however, only in recent years that work in Great Britain on the problems of the gifted has grown in any marked degree, notwithstanding the early interest of scholars like Burt. Most of the books mentioned in this chapter are, therefore, American and those which discuss practical problems, such as those of curriculum and methods of teaching, do so in the context of American education. Some re-interpretation by non-American readers will be necessary from time to time to allow for different organization and practice in education in other countries. Much valuable research has been reported in articles in journals, but the suggestions which follow are confined to books in order to limit their number and because the wider scope of a book is more useful in an early reconnaisance of the field. Readers will find articles listed in the bibliographies of the books mentioned. The selection must not be taken to imply that the books included in it are in some way superior to others; they are mentioned as examples of work in the different categories. The categories, themselves, are arbitrary and are devised for the convenience of a reader wishing to start with a particular topic. There is a good deal of overlapping; some books mentioned in one category might justifiably have been placed in another but this seems to be inevitable when any division is attempted.

Compilations and bibliographies

A good way of sampling contributions to different aspects of the study of giftedness is by dipping into collections of extracts from

H

research reports or chapters specially written by experts. In America, the National Society for the Study of Education devoted yearbooks (1924, 1958) to the gifted and, between 1957 and 1960, in conjunction with associations for the study of particular subjects, published books on those subjects for gifted children in secondary schools. Witty (1951) edited a well-known book for the American Association for Gifted Children which contains a summary of the Stanford studies of Terman and Oden and a chapter on the work of Hollingworth. Other topics include special provision for the gifted in science and the arts and the book concludes with a classified and very fully annotated bibliography. In Great Britain, for two successive years, the *Yearbook of Education* (1961, 1962) was concerned with the gifted and its articles on a wide variety of topics offer a useful view of the extent of the field and some acquaintance with work being done in different countries. Another well-known compilation is that made by French (1966) in which the articles, mostly from professional journals, are divided into categories: identifying characteristics, conditions productive of academic talent, school provision from kindergarten to college, under-achievement, guidance, creativity, state of research and evaluation. It is a radical revision of its 1959 predecessor, the original articles being almost wholly replaced by a smaller number of more recent ones and the introductory material expanded. The book has no bibliography, but references are given at the ends of sections. Another valuable and more recent book of readings, Gowan and Torrance (1971), contains thirty-three extracts and articles, most of which are reprinted from *The Gifted Child Quarterly*. They are grouped in twelve sections covering the usual topics, such as characteristics, curriculum, guidance, teachers, parents and, more unusual, disadvantaged gifted youth. Each section has a short introduction and the book concludes with a bibliography of books and articles, nearly all of which appeared during the previous ten years. Gowan (1961) also compiled a useful and well organized annotated bibliography of selected research in the ten years preceding its publication. It contains more than 700 items, alphabetically arranged, indexed by subjects, and the subjects then indexed alphabetically. In Great Britain, an annotated bibliography of selected items (Start, 1972) has been compiled for the National Foundation for Educational Research.

General studies

Recent years have seen the publication of a large number of general studies of the gifted, as distinct from those reporting on particular investigations or projects. An earlier one by De Haan and Havighurst (1957) is a general introductory text-book for teachers based on the authors' work, then in progress, with the Quincy, Illinois youth development project. It also draws examples from a survey of programmes for the gifted. Topics covered include identification and meeting the child's needs in home, school and community. There is also a bibliography of selected items, classified by topics, with a short note describing each item. Abraham (1958) provides a popular introduction for the general reader interested in the problems of the gifted and what can be done about them by parents, schools, teachers and the community. The book contains a selected bibliography, usefully annotated. Freehill (1961) covers topics ranging from the nature of giftedness, its identification and attitudes towards it, to programme planning and parent-teacher co-operation. The discussion of the nature of giftedness and of curriculum and method occupy the major part of the book. There is also a useful survey of different kinds of provision made for gifted children. There is no bibliography but references are given in footnotes. In spite of its title, which might be misleading to a teacher in Great Britain, a book by Durr (1964) makes many suggestions for educational techniques and school programmes for the use of teachers of the gifted at elementary and secondary levels. The emphasis throughout is on practical suggestions and, although there is no bibliography, there are lists of references at the ends of chapters. Another book on teaching is by Gallagher (1964). Gold (1965) aims to relate research and practice in actual situations to problems in the education of the gifted. His range of topics is wide, including intelligence testing, creativity, planning programmes for the gifted, teaching 'thinking', language arts, science and mathematics, fine arts, ability grouping, motivation and under-achievement, and research. An extensive bibliography concludes a well arranged and informative book. A book, published in Great Britain, for the general reader about the problems of gifted children is by Branch and Cash (1966). One of the authors, Mrs Margaret Branch, is hon. general secretary of the National Association for Gifted Children. This book contains a number of descriptions of individual children as examples of the problems discussed and refers to work currently in progress. In a recent work by Rice (1970) the discussion of the development and administration of special programmes gains significance from the fact that the author had had first-hand experience of one of them as co-director of the California Project Talent which was developed in conjunction with Sacramento State College. The spread of provision is indicated by the report that, by 1965, eleven States had assigned at least one full-time consultant to be responsible for talent development programmes. Others had appointed part-time consultants, but there were still twenty-one States doing little or nothing. The usual topics are also covered in the book and there is an extensive bibliography.

Biographical, longitudinal and special studies

The work of Galton (1869) is generally regarded as a pioneer in the analysis of human ability. A biographical study of the achievements of eminent families led him to the view that intellectual ability is chiefly inherited and was the stimulus for much subsequent work on the nature of genius. The theme was taken up, after the turn of the century by Ellis (1904) and an interesting large scale biographical investigation was, later, undertaken by Cox (1926). A vast amount of information was assembled about the early mental development of 300 intellectually eminent historical persons and was then examined by psychologists to arrive at an estimated minimum IQ for each. This led to the conclusion that had IQ tests been available, the subjects would have been classed as gifted when children. It did not follow from this that gifted children would always become outstanding adults, because traits of personality, such as persistence and drive, have to be taken into account. A different approach, studying physique and temperament, was made by Kretschmer (1931). An example of the biographical study of eminence in a particular field is found in the case studies of well-known scientists, made by Roe (1952). The Goertzels (1965) classify their summarized biographies according to the different kinds of early environment of the subjects. The Illingworths (1966) examine the childhood of exceptional men and women for light on such topics as precocity, learning difficulties and unrecognized ability.

   On-going, observational studies of development over long periods of time are, for obvious reasons, difficult to carry through, and that begun by Terman in 1921 is unique. His study of some 1,500 children of IQ 140 and above (Terman, 1925) was continued to their middle life (Terman and Oden, 1947 and 1959), with a follow-up after forty years by Oden (1968). Other, less ambitious, follow-up studies include one by Sumption (1941) of the subsequent development of gifted children who had been in the special classes in Cleveland, Ohio. As the time span of longitudinal, or follow-up, studies shortens they shade off into the much larger number of special studies of the social and psychological aspects of giftedness. One of these (Hollingworth, 1942) furnished data on the difficulties in social adjustment of children of very high IQ. In New Zealand, Parkyn (1948) studied three groups of children described as highly intelligent and gathered data on their scholastic performance, interests and home backgrounds. In Great Britain, a useful, short study by Shields (1968), based on research covers the problem of definition, characteristics of giftedness, creativity, logical thinking, and educating the gifted child. A list of references is given at the end of each chapter. A notable special study of 103 intelligent children with learning or behaviour difficulties, referred for examination between 1956 and 1961, has been reported by Kellmer Pringle (1970). The book contains case studies illustrating the effects of too high or too low parental expectations, emotional stress in the home, and physical handicap. Data from the examinations of the children are presented and there are sections on learning and adjustment and the practical implications of the study for future action. Finally, a book for the general reader (Deakin, 1972), which describes the unusual upbringing of a family of gifted children, will be found interesting.

Projects

One of the most widely known experiments in the education of gifted children is that which was begun in 1941 with the setting up of Hunter College Elementary School in New York. Ten years later, Hildreth (1952) described its work and some of the problems and attempted an assessment of its outcomes in academic achievement, skills and attitudes. The school's organization and aims, programme and methods, relations with parents and community, and role in teacher training were also described. The book contains few references to other work on the gifted and there is no bibliography. Another well-known project, dating from some twenty years earlier than the

Hunter School, is the major work plan in Cleveland, Ohio (Hall, 1956) involving the establishment of special classes. A series of short summaries of some forty-five projects forms the main part of Havighurst, Stivers and De Haan (1955) which also contains an annotated bibliography, classified by topics. A recent survey (Axford, 1971), of special educational facilities for gifted children was commissioned by the International Foundation for Gifted Children. The entries are almost wholly American; those for European countries are very few and, judging by the only two for England, Marlborough and the Yehudi Menuhin School, quite fortuitous. There is a bibliography. In Great Britain, the pioneer work of Brentwood College of Education with young gifted children coming from Essex schools for half a day each week has been reported by Bridges (1969). This book contains an account of the experiment followed by chapters on the teaching of different subjects and a bibliography.

Curriculum and method

The main source of suggestions on the curriculum and methods of teaching gifted children is to be found in general works, compilations and those describing particular educational projects. The present widespread interest in curriculum development is also producing quantities of material, some of which is suitable, or can be adapted, for clever children. Three books, specially concerned with curriculum and method for the gifted, may, however, be mentioned. Fliegler (1961) is the editor of a book containing chapters on subjects in the curriculum by various writers. Torrance (1965) contains general chapters on identification and motivation, but deals mainly with principles of curriculum development and methods of teaching applicable to kindergarten and elementary ages. Thus, there are chapters on setting the stage in kindergarten, helping gifted children to become creative readers, and developing research concepts and skills, followed by a list of references. Another useful and practical book on curriculum and method is that by Martinson (1968) which discusses meeting the needs of gifted children individually and in groups and planning the work in different subjects such as social studies, mathematics and science, language, music and art. The book ends with a note on the evaluation of programmes and contains a selected bibliography.

Divergent thinking or creativity

Although the books suggested in this section are not specifically on gifted children, they are included because of the recent rapid growth in interest in divergent thinking, or creativity as it is often called, in the gifted. Much of the research has been reported in professional journals and a convenient way of becoming acquainted with its range and some of its authors is by examining compilations. For readers in Great Britain, Vernon (1970) is recent, comprehensive and readily accessible. The range of extracts is wide and the authors representative. There are also suggestions for further reading. A few only, of the many American collections of readings can be given. Anderson (1959) contains an article on traits of creativity by Guilford, whose presidential address in 1950 to the American Psychological Association is generally thought to mark the beginning of recent research on creativity. An article in Smith (1959) analyses over one hundred definitions of creativity and Gruber (1962) contains an important article by McClelland on physical scientists. Creativity in science is also the theme of Taylor and Barron (1963). Two other collections made by Taylor (1964) and two more recent ones by Kagan (1967) and Mooney and Razik (1967) may also be mentioned.

Among books reporting research on creativity one of the best known in recent years is by Getzels and Jackson (1962) describing their work with adolescents in Chicago whose divergent thinking ability they measured with a battery of 'open-ended' tests. Another well-known investigator in this field is Torrance (1962, 1963) who began with studies confirming the work of Getzels and Jackson and went on to apply them to education, particularly at the elementary level. One of his studies (1965) is concerned with the teacher's attitude to the creative pupil. The relationship between general intelligence and creativity was examined by Wallach and Kogan (1965). A good deal of work on divergent thinking has been done by Hudson (1968a) who reports interesting personality studies of 'convergers' and 'divergers'.

Bibliography

ABRAHAM, W. (1958), *Common Sense about Gifted Children*, Harper, New York.

ANDERSON, H. H. (ed.) (1959), *Creativity and its Cultivation*, Harper, New York.

ANDERSON, H. H. (ed.) (1965), *Creativity in Childhood and Adolescence*, Science & Behavior Books, Palo Alto, California.

AXFORD, L. B. (1971), *A Directory of Educational Programs for the Gifted*, Scarecrow Press, Metuchen, New Jersey.

BISHOP, W. E. (1968), 'Successful teachers of the gifted', *Exceptional Children*, 34, 317–25.

BRANCH, M. and CASH, A. (1966), *Recognising and Developing Educational Ability*, Souvenir Press, London.

BRIDGES, S. A. (ed.) (1969), *Gifted Children and the Brentwood Experiment*, Pitman, London.

COX, C. M. (1926), *Genetic Studies of Genius*, vol. 2: *The Early Mental Traits of Three Hundred Geniuses*, Stanford University Press, California.

DEAKIN, M. (1972), *The Children on the Hill: The Story of an Extraordinary Family*, André Deutsch, London.

DE HAAN, R. F. and HAVIGHURST, R. J. (1957), *Educating Gifted Children*, University of Chicago Press.

DURR, W. K. (1964), *The Gifted Student*, Oxford University Press, New York.

ELLIS, H. (1904), *A Study of British Genius*, Hurst & Blackett, London.

FLIEGLER, L. A. (ed.) (1961), *Curriculum Planning for the Gifted*, Prentice-Hall, Englewood Cliffs, New Jersey.

FREEHILL, M. F. (1961), *Gifted Children: Their Psychology and Education*, Macmillan, New York.

FRENCH, J. L. (ed.) (1966), *Educating the Gifted: A Book of Readings*, Holt Rinehart & Winston, New York.

FRIERSON, E. C. (1968), 'The gifted' in Johnson, G. O. and Blank, H. D., *Exceptional Children Research Review*, Council for Exceptional Children, Washington D.C.

GALLAGHER, J. J. (1964), *Teaching the Gifted Child*, Allyn & Bacon, Boston.

GALLAGHER, J. J. (ed.) (1968), *Teaching Gifted Students: A Book of Readings*, Allyn & Bacon, Boston.

GALLAGHER, J. J., ASCHNER, M. J. and JENNÉ, W. (1967), *Productive Thinking of Gifted Children in Classroom Interaction*, Council for Exceptional Children, Washington, D.C.

GALTON, F. (1869), *Hereditary Genius*, Macmillan, London.

GARDNER, M. (1966), *More Mathematical Puzzles and Diversions*, Penguin Books, Harmondsworth.

GETZELS, J. W. and JACKSON, B. W. (1962), *Creativity and Intelligence*, Wiley, New York.

GHISELIN, B. (ed.) (1955), *The Creative Process*, Mentor, New York.

GOERTZEL, V. and GOERTZEL, M. G. (1965), *Cradles of Eminence*, Constable, London.

GOLD, M. J. (1965), *Education of the Intellectually Gifted*, Charles E. Merrill Books, Columbus, Ohio.

GOWAN, J. C. (1961), *An Annotated Bibliography on the Academically Talented*, National Education Association, Washington, D.C.

GOWAN, J. C., DEMOS, G. D. and TORRANCE, E. P. (eds) (1967), *Creativity: Its Educational Implications*, Wiley, New York.

GOWAN, J. C. and TORRANCE, E. P. (eds) (1971), *Educating the Ablest*, Peacock, Itasca, Illinois.

GRUBER, H. E., TERRELL, G. and WERTHEIMER, M. (eds) (1962), *Contemporary Approaches to Creative Thinking*, Atherton Press, New York.

HALL, T. (1956), *Gifted Children: The Cleveland Story*, World Publishing Co., Cleveland.

HAVIGHURST, R. J., STIVERS, E. and DE HAAN, R. F. (1955), *A Survey of the Education of Gifted Children*, University of Chicago Press.

HILDRETH, G. H. (1966), *Introduction to the Gifted*, McGraw-Hill, New York.

HILDRETH, G. H. *et al.* (1952), *Educating Gifted Children at Hunter College Elementary School*, Harper, New York.

HOLLINGWORTH, L. S. (1926), *Gifted Children: Their Nature and Nurture*, Macmillan, New York.

HOLLINGWORTH, L. S. (1942), *Children who tested Above 180 I.Q. Stanford-Binet: Origin and Development*, World Book Co., New York.

HUDSON, L. (1968a), *Contrary Imaginations*, Penguin Books, Harmondsworth.

HUDSON, L. (1968b), *Frames of Mind*, Methuen, London.

ILLINGWORTH, R. S. and ILLINGWORTH, C. M. (1966), *Lessons from Childhood: Some Aspects of the Early Life of Unusual Men and Women*, Livingstone, Edinburgh.

KAGAN, J. (ed.) (1967), *Creativity and Learning*, Houghton Mifflin, Boston.

KRETSCHMER, E. (1931), *The Psychology of Men of Genius*, Kegan Paul, London.

LOOMIS, G. I. (1951), *Survey of Literature and Research concerning the Education of the Gifted Child*, School of Education, University of Oregon.

LUCITO, L. J. (1963), 'Gifted children' in Dunn, L. M. (ed.), *Exceptional Children in the Schools*, Holt, Rinehart & Winston, New York.

MARTINSON, R. A. (1968), *Curriculum Enrichment for the Gifted in the Primary Grades*, Prentice-Hall, Englewood Cliffs, New Jersey.

MOONEY, R. L. and RAZIK, T. A. (eds) (1967), *Explorations in Creativity*, Harper & Row, New York.

MYERS, R. E. (1961), *An Experimental Program in Creative Thinking*, University of Minnesota Bureau of Educational Research, Minneapolis.

NATIONAL SOCIETY FOR THE STUDY OF EDUCATION (1924), *The Education of Gifted Children*, Twenty-third Yearbook part 1, Public School Publishing Co., Bloomington, Illinois.

NATIONAL SOCIETY FOR THE STUDY OF EDUCATION (1958), *Education for the Gifted*, Fifty-seventh Yearbook, part 2, University of Chicago Press.

ODEN, M. H. (1968), 'The fulfilment of promise: 40 year follow-up of the Terman gifted group', *Genetic Psychology Monographs*, 77.

PARKYN, G. W. (1948), *Children of High Intelligence: A New Zealand Study*, New Zealand Council for Educational Research, Oxford University Press, London.

PARNES, S. J. and HARDING, H. F. (1962), *A Source Book for Creative Thinking*, Scribner, New York.

PEEL, E. A. (1967), *The Pupil's Thinking*, Oldbourne Book Co., London.

PEGNATO, C. V. and BIRCH, J. W. (1966), 'Locating gifted children in junior high schools—a comparison of methods' in French, J. L. (ed.), *Educating the Gifted: A Book of Readings*, Holt, Rinehart & Winston, New York.

PRINGLE, M. L. KELLMER (1970), *Able Misfits: A study of educational and behaviour difficulties of 103 very intelligent children (I.Q.s 120–200)*, Longman, London.

REYNOLDS, M. C. (1962), *Early School Admission for Mentally Advanced Children*, Council for Exceptional Children, Washington, D.C.

RICE, J. P. (1970), *The Gifted: Developing Total Talent*, Charles C. Thomas, Springfield, Illinois.

ROE, A. (1952), *The Making of a Scientist*, Dodd Mead, New York.

SCHOENFELD, C. (1970), 'Towards a national strategy for environmental education', *Journal of Educational Research*, 64, 1.

SCHWAB, J. J. (1969), 'The practical: a language for curriculum', *School Review*, 78, 1–23.

SHIELDS, J. B. (1968), *The Gifted Child*, National Foundation for Educational Research, Slough, Bucks.

SMITH, P. (ed.) (1959), *Creativity: An Examination of the Creative Process*, Hastings House, New York.

SPAULDING, R. L. (1968), 'What teacher attributes bring out the best in gifted children? Affective dimensions of creative processes' in Gallagher, J. J. (ed.), *Teaching Gifted Students: A Book of Readings*, Allyn & Bacon, Boston.

START, A. (1972), *The Gifted Child: A Select, Annotated Bibliography*, National Foundation for Educational Research, Slough, Bucks.

STEIN, M. I. and HEINZE, S. J. (1960), *Creativity and the Individual*, Free Press, Chicago.

SUMPTION, M. R. (1941), *Three Hundred Gifted Children*, World Book Co., New York.

TAYLOR, C. W. (ed.) (1964), *Creativity: Progress and Potential*, McGraw-Hill, New York.

TAYLOR, C. W. (ed.) (1964), *Widening Horizons in Creativity*, Wiley, New York.

TAYLOR, C. W. and BARRON, F. (1963), *Scientific Creativity: Its Recognition and Development*, Wiley, New York.

TAYLOR, C. W. and WILLIAMS, F. E. (1966), *Instructional Media and Creativity*, Wiley, New York.

TAYLOR, P. M. (1970), *How Teachers Plan their Courses*, National Foundation for Educational Research, Slough, Bucks.

TERMAN, L. M. *et al.* (1925), *Genetic Studies of Genius, vol. 1: Mental and Physical Traits of a Thousand Gifted Children*, Stanford University Press, California.

TERMAN, L. M. and ODEN, M. H. (1947), *Genetic Studies of Genius, vol. 4: The Gifted Child Grows Up*, Stanford University Press, California.

TERMAN, L. M. and ODEN, M. H. (1959), *Genetic Studies of Genius, vol. 5: The Gifted Group at Mid-Life*, Stanford University Press, California.

TORRANCE, E. P. (1962), *Guiding Creative Talent*, Prentice-Hall, Englewood Cliffs, New Jersey.

TORRANCE, E. P. (1963), *Education and the Creative Potential*, University of Minnesota Press, Minneapolis.

TORRANCE, E. P. (1965), *Gifted Children in the Classroom*, Macmillan, New York.

TORRANCE, E. P. (ed.) (1960), *Talent and Education*, University of Minnesota Press, Minneapolis.

VERNON, P. E. (ed.) (1970), *Creativity: Selected Readings*, Penguin Books, Harmondsworth.

WALLACH, M. A. and KOGAN, N. (1965), *Modes of Thinking in Young Children: A Study of the Creativity-Intelligence Distinction*, Holt, Rinehart & Winston, New York.

WALLACH, M. A. and WING, C. W. Jr (1969), *The Talented Student*, Holt, Rinehart & Winston, New York.

WARD, W. C. (1968), 'Creativity in young children', *Child Development*, 39, 737–54.

WING, H. (1968), *Tests of Musical Ability and Appreciation*, British Journal of Psychology Monograph Supplement, Cambridge University Press.

WITTY, P. (ed.) (1951), *The Gifted Child*, American Association for Gifted Children, Heath, Boston.

YEARBOOK OF EDUCATION (1961), *Concepts of Excellence in Education*, Evans, London.

YEARBOOK OF EDUCATION (1962), *The Gifted Child*, Evans, London.

YOUNG, D. (1966), *Non-Readers Intelligence Test*, University of London Press.

Index